Isabel de Villena
Portraits of Holy Women

Isabel de Villena
Portraits of Holy Women
Selections from the
Vita Christi

Introduction and selection of texts by
Joan Curbet

Translation and notes by
Robert D. Hughes

BARCINO·TAMESIS
BARCELONA/WOODBRIDGE 2013

First published 2013
by Tamesis (Serie B: TEXTOS, 56)
in association with Editorial Barcino

LLLL institut
ramon llull
Catalan Language and Culture

The translation of this work has been supported
by a grant from the Institut Ramon Llull

ISBN 978 1 85566 259 9
COPYRIGHT DEPOSIT: B. 4456-2013

Tamesis is an imprint of Boydell & Brewer Ltd
PO Box 9, Woodbridge, Suffolk IP12 3DF, UK
and of Boydell & Brewer Inc.
668 Mt Hope Avenue, Rochester, NY 14620, USA
www.boydellandbrewer.com

Editorial Barcino, S. A.
Acàcies 15. 08027 Barcelona, Spain
www.editorialbarcino.cat

Designed and typeset by Jordi Casas

Printed in Spain by Gràfiko

Cover illustration:
Anonymous, *Scenes from the life of the Virgin Mary*
Detail of the altar frontal from Avià (Santa Maria
d'Avià, Berguedà, Catalonia)
Beginning of the thirteenth century
© MNAC - Museu Nacional d'Art de Catalunya
Barcelona, 2013
Foto: Calveras/Mérida/Sagristà

84760156 8

Contents

PART TWO: WOMEN DURING THE APOSTOLIC LIFE OF CHRIST

PART THREE: AFTER THE DEATH OF CHRIST

Introduction

I. A WOMAN'S AUTHORITY, A WOMAN'S VOICE

AT SOME POINT in the month of March 1497, in the monastery of the Holy Trinity in Valencia, the abbess Aldonça de Montsoriu added a small introductory note and some brief concluding remarks to a long manuscript she was preparing for print: that material was a Life of Christ (*Vita Christi*) which had been written in the vernacular tongue by her predecessor, Sor (i.e. Sister) Isabel de Villena. To the best of our knowledge, this is the only major literary work in Catalan to have been written by a woman in the late-Middle Ages: its very existence constitutes an extraordinary exception, and the circumstances in which it came to print deserve our attention as well. Sister Aldonça presents the act of publication as a response to external inquiries that had reached the monastery, coming from none other than Queen Isabel of Castile, whom she addresses directly:

> The resplendent light of devotion that shines within Your Highness has revealed to you that in this your monastery a devout *Vita Christi* had been set in order by the illustrious Lady Elionor, otherwise known as Sister Isabel de Villena, our Reverend Abbess and our Mother; and because Your Royal Excellency, wholly inflamed with love of the great King of Paradise, had written to ask the General Bailiff of this your kingdom of Valencia to send you a copy of that work, I intend to perform this welcome service for Your Majesty, so that it might reach your royal hands sooner, by having that work printed (p. 43)[1]

---

[1] All the quotations from the *Vita Christi* and of its paratexts are drawn from Robert D. Hughes's translation in the present edition.

By presenting the act of publication as a response to the Queen's devotion, Aldonça inadvertently indicates to us, twenty-first century readers, how close the text came to having remained in manuscript form, its circulation mostly restricted to the nuns to whom it was addressed, and probably reaching a few select members of the Valencian lay society of the period. A sequence of external interventions, stretching from the Queen to the Bailiff to Aldonça, has impacted upon the text and projected it outwards: the shift from manuscript to print corresponds here to a shift from the monastic sphere (even if it was as prestigious as that of the Trinity monastery) to the world at large, from its initial enclosure to the public arena. It is especially important to observe what this implies in terms of authorial intention, and of the representation thereof; for after all, and according to Aldonça, Isabel de Villena herself had never envisaged or desired this kind of public projection:

> The virtuous and most honourable Mother Abbess, my predecessor, considering by the light of her clear understanding the dangers that worldly praise brings, had descended to such innermost depths of humility that she did not wish to write her name in any part of this book [...]. And since she, a humble nun, is praised for having kept her name silent when composing such a worthy book, I believe myself, as a result, to achieve no small merit before God by divulging the name of such a singular Mother, worthy as she is of immortal memory: Sister Isabel de Villena wrote it; Sister Isabel de Villena composed it; Sister Isabel de Villena, in an elegant and gentle style, lent order to it, not only for the devout sisters and the daughters of obedience who inhabit the closed house of this monastery, but also for all those who live during this brief, irksome and transitory life (pp. 43-44).

Aldonça herself appears as a privileged mediator between the original author and the reading public, since it is only through her that the text will be known by a large audience (the Queen herself, of course, sitting at its head): because of her close proximity to the author and her knowledge of the latter's intentions, her self-appointed role is to a certain extent similar to that which scribes all throughout Europe had often adopted in their relation to women writers, before the widespread use of print. The strategy of legitimation at work here is more complex, however: Aldonça firmly insists upon the author's original wish to remain unknown, upon her self-assumed anonymity, in order to define the moral position she had held towards her own work: Sor Isabel's aim was apostolic and didactic rather than self-serving; recognition was not important for her. And yet, it is precisely that self-effacing attitude which finally enables and encourages Aldonça to openly proclaim her name and to endow it with full authority before the reading public: 'Sister Isabel de Villena wrote it; Sister Isabel de Villena composed it; Sister Isabel de Villena, in an elegant and gentle style, lent order to it [...].' In a paradox fully representative of the problematic status of medieval women writers, *humilitas* produces *auctoritas*: from Aldonça's perspective, it is precisely this willingness to disappear in the eyes of the world (an attitude which was in itself a requisite of conventual life) that makes Sister Isabel more deserving of her name's being posthumously recognised and honoured in print.

What occurs in the dedicatory note of the *Vita Christi* is quite typical of the complex strategies whereby the voice of a woman might be allowed to enter the public sphere and claim a place therein during the fifteenth century. Female authorship has been affirmed here through a clever manipulation of the mechanisms (e.g. the association of women with humility, the injunction to silence) that generally worked to suppress it within the context of late-medieval culture; perhaps inadvertently, Sister Aldonça offers a minor instance of a major modus operandi employed in the pages of the *Vita Christi* itself. What Isabel de Villena achieves in her work (and what constitutes one of its most significant claims to relevance in our own period) is a forceful and determined assertion of the capacities of women that, while partly accepting the gender divisions of its period, gently subverts them and modifies them from within, enabling the depiction of fully formed, complex and living female subjects. Quite remarkably, all of this is achieved without the author's ever losing sight of her main aim, which is none other than re-telling the life of Christ so as to bring its full significance before her readers: a crucial and defining aspect of her voice is precisely its deep sensitivity to the multiple connections existing between the feminine and the sacred. We shall be exploring the nature of those connections, and the multiple implications that Sor Isabel draws therefrom in the pages to follow.

II. A MONASTIC LIFE

Any approach to a literary text by a medieval woman must begin by properly placing it within the historical and biographical context of its author, so as to ascertain the initial conditions within which it was produced and the pressures (or freedom) experienced by its author at the time of its composition. A brief survey of the life of Isabel de Villena will enable us to situate the *Vita Christi* as the product of a specific monastic culture located within an active and dynamic urban environment: a privileged point of convergence apt to fall under the influence of forces emanating from both the secular and the ecclesiastical realms.

Sor Isabel's father, Enrique de Villena (1384-1434), was a remarkable though troubled and problematic figure. A nobleman initially favoured by the kings of Castile, who organised his advantageous marriage to Maria de Albornoz in 1401, he nevertheless sought the annulment of this union only three years afterwards, so as to enter the military Order of Calatrava; he was eventually granted the title of Grand Master thereof in 1405, and he managed to obtain this exceptional position while remaining a secular member, without having had to enter the novitiate. These were risky and unusual movements for an aristocrat of his rank, and in later years they would be acknowledged as being entirely characteristic of his unpredictable personality. His authority as Master of the order was repeatedly questioned both by religious and secular authorities of the highest rank, and he was ultimately forced to renounce it in 1412; documentary evidence concerning the case proves beyond doubt that he had only managed to maintain this position as a result of the direct intervention and protection of King Martin of Aragon. Enrique's genuine strengths and interests lay elsewhere, in the areas of scholarship and literature in which he always excelled: he participated directly in the organisation and promotion of literary contests in Barcelona and Valencia, where he became a major force in cultural affairs; clearly it was his proficiency in such areas which kept him on good terms with the Aragonese and Castilian monarchs, despite the fact that they were repeatedly disturbed by his uncontrollable tendency towards 'outrages, inappropriate conduct and controversies' (*scándalos, inconvenientes e pleytos*, as King Martin himself defined them in a remarkable letter).[2] It was the direct protection of the Royal House of Aragon that guaranteed a continued stability to Enrique in spite of his troublesome personality, and which granted him the resources enabling him to complete a significant poetic output throughout the 1410s and 20s, a corpus which includes a treatise on poetry such as the *Arte de trovar* ('The Art of Versification') and a mythographic account such as *Los dotze treballs d'Hèrcules* ('The Twelve Labours of Hercules'). The social career of Enrique de Villena seemingly came to an end long before his life: he spent his final years secluded in his library in

---

[2] Quoted by Albert-Guillem Hauf i Valls, in Isabel de Villena, *Vita Christi*, Barcelona, Edicions 62 i La Caixa (Les Millors Obres de la Literatura Catalana, 115), 1995, p. 9.

Cuenca and entirely devoted to literature and scholarship, until his death in 1434; his illegitimate daughter, Elionor Manuel (whom we know under her adopted name as a nun, namely, Isabel), had been born four years before.

The young Elionor probably spent a large part of her childhood and adolescence in the royal palace of the kings of Aragon, as a direct protégée of Queen Maria of Aragon, who would give her continuous support during the early years of her life. Within this context she found herself in a paradoxical position: on the one hand she was at the heart of a rich centre of power and culture, and enjoyed the immediate influence of a courtly entourage that prided itself on its literary and artistic sophistication; on the other, and as an illegitimate daughter, she was cut off from any hope of fully legitimising her position within such a context. Doubtless she received a solid education: as a young lady who lived under the direct protection of the monarchy, she must at least have acquired a good knowledge of the *trivium* in her formative years, and the plentiful library of Queen Maria must have been open to her at all times. At a more mature age (and as the text of the *Vita Christi* itself attests), her mastery of Latin and of the traditions of biblical commentary became thoroughgoing indeed, although we can only speculate on the extent to which her training in those particular fields had begun within a courtly setting; it is logical to think, at any rate, that such developments must have drawn early succour from her initial contact with secular literature. Her destiny was, quite inevitably, a religious life: no other option was available to the illegitimate daughter of a powerful nobleman. As a consequence, she took her first vows as a convent novice in early 1445; she was, in fact, entering a community of Poor Clares that would later establish itself, thanks to the direct supervision and patronage of Queen Maria, in the newly-built monastery of the Holy Trinity.

What is beyond doubt is that, for Isabel (as she was now known), conventual life certainly did not imply social exclusion or inactivity: on the contrary, her progress within the monastery allowed her to become one of the dominant figures in the social and ecclesiastic world of late-fifteenth-century Valencia. The very text of the *Vita Christi*, oriented as it is towards the spiritual instruction of nuns (and, therefore, towards a primarily didactic purpose), may legitimately be taken as indicative of an active, self-conscious and communicative personality: its very composition must have been part of a wider literary activity undertaken by Sor Isabel, an activity which had the convent as both its focus and its principal—although probably not exclusive—audience. In 1462, when she was in her

early thirties and after seventeen years of religious life, she became the
abbess of the Trinity convent: from that moment on and for the following
twenty-eight years, direct references and allusions to her recur constantly
in both official and private documents within Valencian civic life. Her functions as an abbess necessarily gave her a strong institutional position, both
within and without the convent: within, as a leader and guide, endowed
with the capacity to address and supervise the life of the group; and without, as a mediator of its demands and needs before the civil and ecclesiastical authorities. Both aspects required the development of a sense of lead-
ership and of a strong individual voice: a complex and demanding position, which could not have been maintained for decades without a clear
awareness of the empowerment it implied.

Her institutional role was certainly not restricted to spiritual matters.
The abbess of a large convent, especially in a rich and prosperous urban
area, was directly responsible for the material welfare of the institution
and for its continued presence and influence in its immediate environment. In this respect, the economic and architectural history of the Trinity monastery bears witness to Sor Isabel's ability to sustain and increase
the frequency of external donations, with large quantities being invested
in its protracted construction: entire sections of the building were initi-
ated under her administration, including the cloisters, the external
porches and doorways, the stained-glass windows and the floor of the
church. Practically all of the important figures and families in Valencia
made donations towards the completion of the building: among them,
and from a purely literary perspective, it is important to notice the presence of major writers such as Ausiàs March, Joan Roís de Corella and
Jaume Roig. Most of them must have been in direct personal contact with
sister Isabel at one point or another: all throughout these years, the notion
of *urbanitas* and the social skills she must have acquired as a child under
the protection of Queen Maria were put to excellent use. Several documents from the period allow us to gauge her position: the warm and com-
plimentary letters addressed to her by notable lay poets, as well as the ded-
ications to her which feature in books written by the bishop Jaume Péreç,[3]
indicate that she had acquired the highest possible level of prominence
to which a woman could aspire in her times. It is impossible to determine,
however, the precise extent to which Sor Isabel remained aware of the new

---

[3] Quoted by Josep Almiñana i Vallés, in Isabel de Villena, *Vita Christi*, 2 vols.,
Valencia, Ajuntament de València, 1992, Vol. 1, pp. 149-150.

literary developments taking place in the world of the Court and of the city, although it is equally impossible that she could have remained unaware of them; some of her writings on spiritual contemplation may also have circulated outside of the monastery.

In 1484 Sor Isabel became the tutor to one of King Ferdinand's illegitimate daughters, who entered the Trinity convent: while this circumstance probably marked the apogee of the former's social position and respectability, it also ensured that the convent would continue to benefit from the protection of the Castilian-Aragonese monarchy even after her death, which occurred in 1490. Her ecclesiastical career had been productive and prestigious: however, its prerogatives also dictated that her literary work should be restricted to spirituality and that it tended to circulate, during her lifetime, within the monastic contexts in which, and for which, it had been conceived. In the end, it was precisely Sor Isabel's lifelong association with royalty that allowed the *Vita Christi* to transcend the limitations of manuscript transmission: Queen Isabel of Castile, coming to hear of its existence and of the great devotion that lay behind it, made some inquiries thereabout which led the then abbess, Aldonça de Montsoriu, to bring the lengthy work to print: this, at least, is what Aldonça herself stated in the brief dedication to the Queen which prefaces the first edition of the *Vita* in 1497, seven years after Sor Isabel's death.

Besides the *Vita Christi*, it is not possible to attribute any other literary work to Sor Isabel; there have been, however, several scholarly attempts to clarify her possible authorship with respect to certain manuscript works which were produced in or around her lifetime, and which have been documented as forming part of the monastery's library during the fifteenth century.[4] One of these, a work called the *Speculum animae*, which consists of a series of illuminations depicting the life and Passion of Christ, was clearly used by the nuns in their devotional exercises; these illuminations are supplemented in the manuscript by a series of commentaries which encourage contemplation in terms that must be set within the same tradition to which the *Vita Christi* belongs. Even though it has not been possible to determine the specific relationship between this text and Sor Isabel's own work, its mere presence in the monastery attests to the strong influence that the practice of Franciscan affective spirituality exerted upon the latter, and encourages us to situate the *Vita*

---

[4] On the problematic attribution of these works, see Hauf, *op. cit.*, pp. 24-26 and 31-33.

Christi itself firmly within that particular tradition. It is also worth mentioning that one mid-fifteenth-century manuscript which includes a *Tractat de la Passió a manera de sermó* ('Treatise on the Passion in the Form of a Sermon') contains a great deal of textual material which also appears in the *Vita Christi*. It has not been possible to establish clearly whether this text was completed before or after the *Vita*, or what kind of part (authorial or indirect) Sor Isabel played in it: a likely possibility is that the *Sermon* was completed by Sor Isabel herself before her appointment as abbess, and that she later used it as a first draft for her much longer work, but even that possibility remains uncertain. None of these works of dubious attribution detract from the fact that her authorship and control over the *Vita* was direct, and it is on the strength of this work that her position in Catalan literature, and in late medieval culture as a whole, must be assessed. If the voice of Isabel de Villena continues to be relevant today it is because, in her patient dedication to her work, she was able to find a distinctive voice of her own: a woman's voice that casts itself over the domains of the physical and of the spiritual, and which is deeply aware of the close interconnections between both.

III. The *Vita Christi* and the tradition of affective spirituality

No major literary achievement ever occurs in a vacuum: rather, it tends to be the result of a creative readaptation of previously existing materials. Seen from a historical perspective, the figure of Sor Isabel can legitimately claim a place among the late exponents of a major European tradition: the text of the *Vita Christi* is a unique instance of the affective spirituality that had developed steadily in Europe from the twelfth century onwards, and which had contributed enormously to the development of new forms of subjectivity throughout the late-Middle Ages. A significant part of her achievement lies in the fact that she was able to tap into cultural forms that were solidly established within Western spheres of culture before her own time, and to rewrite and adapt them from a specifically female viewpoint. Before moving onwards, it will be necessary to delineate that context briefly.

The great monastic reformation of the twelfth century had based a great part of its strength upon an innovative approach to the practice of meditation. Under the influence of major preachers and theologians such as Bernard of Clairvaux it was possible to reformulate the very notion of prayer, putting a major emphasis on the emotional link between the individual subject and the human nature of Christ; in itself, this perspective could lay the foundations for a growing feeling of compassion, which would make the soul more receptive to the transcendent significance of the Incarnation. Meditation thus came to be based upon *affectus*, that is, upon the emotional response awakened by the life of Christ itself in its most minute details, its human circumstances and its experience of suffering, all of these leading to the apotheosis of the Resurrection. This is how St. Bernard described the ideal attitude of a receptive subject at prayer:

> The soul at prayer should have before it a sacred image of the God-man, in his birth or infancy or as he was teaching, or dying, or rising, or ascending. Whatever form it takes, this image must bind the soul with the love of virtue and expel carnal vice, eliminate temptations and quiet desires. I think this is the principal reason why the invisible God willed to be seen in the flesh and to converse with men as a man.[5]

Trinitarian hermeneutics can thus become attuned to the needs and demands of the individual believer: he or she must start by considering the humanity of Christ, coming closer to it in emotional terms; the soul is thus made ready to apprehend the sacrificial component of the Incarnation, and thus to move on from the human to the divine, from the understanding of the Son to that of the whole Trinity in its loving relationship with mankind. If this affective connection between the Godhead and humanity is possible, it is because of the bonds that have been established since the dawn of time between the Creator and his creatures: human beings, both male and female, were made in God's image, and the assumption of flesh by the divinity must be seen as a reassertion of that fact. In assuming the form of man, Christ became the perfect instance of the *imago Dei* that had originally been imprinted upon humanity: it was therefore only logical that, through a circular movement, contemplation of his human circumstances should lead gradually to an understanding of his divine nature as the Creator. As St. Anselm of Canterbury put it, summarising this whole process: 'I thank

---

[5] Bernard of Clairvaux, 'Commentary on the Song of Songs', in *Sancti Bernardi Opera*, ed. J. Leclerq, Ch. H. Talbot and H. Rochais, Rome, Editiones Cistercienses, 1957-1958, Vol. 1, p. 118.

you, God, that you created me in your image, that, remembering you, I might think of you and love you.'[6]

What this development involved was no less than a spirituality grounded on the material and psychological conditions experienced by the believers, rather than on an abstract doctrine: a true *theologia cordis*, or theology of the heart. Following this model, meditation on the life of Christ is activated by memory; this in turn leads on to the understanding of its transcendent reality, and the whole process culminates in the full contemplation of the deity. An identification is thus established between the individual subject and the human reality of Christ, strengthening the links between the one and the other: this amounts to developing a capacity to recognise the transcendental within the material; and, simultaneously, to projecting everyday reality onto a higher sphere, effectively learning to 'transcendentalise' it. It was only natural that this tendency should become powerfully linked to developments in Franciscan piety, which from the outset had placed major emphasis on *humilitas* as a means of identification with Christ; and indeed it was in the work produced by members of the Franciscan order that several of these concepts reached their full fruition in the thirteenth century. Several works were produced in this period that contributed towards the expansion of affective spirituality, projecting it outside the monastic institutions and helping it to find a place among laymen and laywomen. A major text in this development was the *Meditationes Vitae Christi* erroneously credited to Saint Bonaventure, which circulated widely in a variety of versions and insisted on the need to introduce the practice of contemplation into the *vita activa*, into the world and into the daily activities of the laity. The text of the *Meditationes* gives the following account of this need:

> Above all the studies of spiritual exercise, I believe this one [i.e. contemplation] is the most necessary and the most fruitful, and the one that may lead to the highest level [...]. Through frequent and continued meditation on His life, the soul attains so much familiarity, confidence and love that it will disdain and disregard other things and be exercised and trained as to what to do and what to avoid.[7]

---

[6] Anselm of Canterbury, *Proslogion*, trans. and introd. M. J. Charlesworth, Oxford, Clarendon Press, 1965, p. 114.

[7] Pseudo-Bonaventure, *Meditations on the Life of Christ*, ed. and trans. I. Ragusa and R. B. Green, Princeton, Princeton University Press, 1961, p. 2.

'Familiarity, confidence and love': these were the key aims of the contemplative in his or her search for close proximity to the sacred, since his or her ultimate desire was nothing less than to draw near to and interact personally with the living Christ. For his part, Saint Bonaventure was the actual author of works such as the *Lignum Vitae*, which also circulated widely, and which insisted on the need to contemplate the labours and the love of the crucified Jesus Christ, always through the vivid representation of the Passion which the praying subject had to keep in his or her mind. Throughout the thirteenth and fourteenth centuries we find similar approaches in the writings of authors influenced in different ways by the Cistercian and Franciscan traditions, authors such as Marguerite d'Oingt, Richard Rolle and Julian of Norwich; all of these works actively encouraged the mental reproduction of scenes of the Passion, or progress towards a visualisation of the final episodes in the life of Christ: imaginative recreation and mental visualisation thus became, throughout Europe, indispensable elements in the practice of contemplation.

Bearing this spiritual tradition in mind, if we now turn to the text of Isabel de Villena's *Vita Christi*, it will become evident that this text can be seen as one of our author's most extraordinary and sophisticated (though belated) literary developments. The very form of the book attests to the aim of furthering and encouraging contemplation. *The Vita* is organised as a series of descriptive vignettes which cover the whole development of the life of Jesus, all of them characterised by an inclusive vocabulary and an effective use of detail, and which gently introduce the reader into their atmosphere, bringing him or her as close as possible to the living reality of the Incarnation and the Holy Family. Moving on from this descriptive level, such sequences open themselves out into lengthy sentences of exaltation and celebration, which are generally uttered by the protagonists themselves: this leads to a loftier style, characterised by an abundant use of superlative adjectival forms and syntactic structures wherein admiration is expressed. Both in terms of the narrative and in terms of the characters therein, emotion thoroughly permeates devotion, but this emotion, far from being an aim in itself, carries with it the understanding of wider doctrinal and theological aspects: in the *Vita Christi*, feeling and knowledge are not opposed, but rather stand in a dialectical and fruitful relation to each other.

A clever and highly idiosyncratic use of adjectives, which in a lesser author would be innocuous or merely functional, is here charged with purpose: what such adjectives evince is an attempt to mediate and guide the subjectivity of the reader, in order to project it onto the object of contemplation while achieving the loftiest possible effect in terms of meaning. The constant recurrence of diminutive terms in the chapters dealing with the childhood of Christ (for instance, diminutives applied to him, to his mother and to their environment; e.g. *petitet, personeta, poquet, doneta,* or in English: 'little one', 'little person', 'little bit', 'little woman') is the sign of a primarily affective discourse: one which approaches not only the characters themselves but the objects which surround them, their clothing and the space they inhabit, with the intention of understanding them emotionally, of appreciating them in their materiality. Such an appreciation then leads to an understanding of the sublimity of the drama being enacted (i.e. the redemption of humanity via the Incarnation), and this motivates the abundance of superlative adjectival forms, or of prepositional clauses, which define the significance of the situations at hand. It is because of this that such vocabulary tends to hover over a paradox: the expression of inexpressibility, the attempt to give verbal form to that which remains always beyond the reach of language. Thus the categories of the 'infinite' or 'boundless', the 'excessive', that which is 'beyond measure' and that 'which cannot be told' (all of them recurring expressions) enter the text in great numbers and function steadily throughout the *Vita Christi* not merely as part of a didactic strategy, but also as an attempt to situate the reader directly in the presence of the sacred, making him or her aware of the transcendent dimension towards which the contemplative process moves.

A large proportion of the stylistic devices employed throughout the *Vita Christi* contribute towards a bridging of the gap that exists between the simple and humble environment in the scenes depicted and the sublime content enacted therein. The interaction between the various voices also has a key role to play here: they must be represented as responding actively and passionately to each other and to the manifestation of the divine among them, so as to achieve the greatest emotional effect on the reader and to elicit an affective response in him or her. This is the reason for the abundant use of exclamations and interjections, the constant use of rhetorical questions (e.g. 'And you, my Lord...?', 'And you, my lady...?', 'And you, my son...?') and the recurrence of the brief vocative address (e.g. 'O lady!', 'O my Lord and my God', 'O my Life!', 'O my daughter!'), spoken by Christ just as much as by the other characters. Such an emphasis on the dramatic exchange among speaking voices must be seen as Sor Isabel's reworking of a major theme within the tradition of affective spirituality: the 'eyewitness-like' nature of the contemplation that must be achieved by the subject at prayer, as he or she *recreates* the biblical scenes in his or her mind. From Bernard of Clairvaux and Saint Bonaventure onwards, the contemplative self had been invited to imagine the key moments of Christ's life in a rich abundance of detail, seeing them and perceiving them in his or her mind as if witnessing them in person. Under optimal conditions, the contemplative subject has to achieve a visual and aural re-enactment of such scenes in the mind, thus facilitating full empathy with the participants therein, as if that subject were participating directly in the situation being evoked. The expressive and emphatic style of the speaking voices within the *Vita Christi* contributes towards an enhancement of this direct involvement: their dynamism creates a sense of living exchange, as if the action were being carried out as a theatrical performance before the reader.

And yet, for all this imaginative recreation and drama, there exists a wealth of biblical erudition and theological discourse informing the textual fabric of the *Vita Christi*. Quotations drawn from the Latin Vulgate reappear in almost every scene (and are uttered by the characters therein) in at least two dominant forms: as sentences taken from the Gospel scenes that are being recreated, and as sentences taken from the Old Testament, the latter being used typologically (i.e. in order to link the Old Testament to the New) so as to underscore the idea of a continuity throughout all sacred history. Sor Isabel's use of this latter kind of fragment is especially relevant, since such fragments assist in displaying the multi-faceted reality of the Incarnation, and the sense of its being the culmination of history. As the exegetical tradition had long established, there was practically no aspect of the life of Christ which had not been highlighted by the voice of God and his prophets within ancient Scripture; both Testaments should be understood as complementing each other at a textual and a transcendent level, the New becoming the fulfilment of the promise contained in the Old. In the *Vita Christi* these typological links tend to be presented explicitly in the voices of the characters themselves, characters who may directly invoke fragments from the Psalms, from Ecclesiasticus or from the Prophets, thus underscoring at every step of the way the idea of completion (i.e. of fulfilment of the ancient, divine promise) that is displayed all throughout Christ's time among men. The presence of the Vulgate text within the *Vita*, however, is not restricted to the Old Testament, nor is its function merely typological: quite often, a basic fragment or sentence from the original Gospel scene being recreated (drawn from Luke, John or Matthew) provides a foundation for the characters' utterances: their voices reproduce key passages from the text that is glossed and expanded by Sor Isabel, displaying openly their scriptural basis and reminding the reader that the roots of this re-elaboration lie in the most sacred ground: Sor Isabel's creative words have the firm support of the Word. Extending beyond biblical texts even, the Latin fragments in the *Vita* also incorporate quotations from the venerable tradition of scriptural commentary, ranging from St. Augustine to St. Bernard of Clairvaux, whose writings Sor Isabel probably knew from their presence in *florilegia* or from anthologies of commonplaces for contemplation. The characters of the *Vita* inhabit a reality that is deeply human yet charged with universal meaning: it is because of this that their language moves between, on the one hand, the fluid representation of their immediate physical and emotional reality and, on the other, the eternally fixed bedrock of Scripture (often quoted directly) and its exegetical tradition.

It will not suffice, therefore, to consider Isabel de Villena's prose as simply being representative of an unspecified kind of women's writing (or, still less, to explain the 'amorous flux' of her prose as the result of her 'feminine condition' or status as a woman)[8] without taking into account the tradition into which she inserts herself. While it is true, as it most certainly is, that she writes unashamedly as a woman, her style is the result of a canny and innovative adaptation of features she had inherited from the rich stream of affective spirituality, and which enabled her to create a dynamic, inclusive voice, capable of encompassing the everyday world as much as theological discourse. The text moves constantly between categories that, in medieval poetics, would have corresponded to the *sermo humilis* and the *sermo gravis*, though it operates with such nimbleness that it contributes towards the erasure of such categories, rendering them ultimately superfluous. In the *Vita Christi*, the lowly and the sublime are always in close proximity to each other (indeed, deeply involved within one another), this being only logical in a work in which the roots of the transcendent are perceived as lying deep within the substance of lived experience, and in which the reader is gently drawn into a constant back-and-forth movement: from biblical quotation to spontaneous exclamation, from the physical to the spiritual, and from the depiction of reality to the perception and understanding of the sacred.

---

[8] Joan Fuster, 'Jacme Roig i Sor Isabel de Villena', in *Obres completes*, Barcelona, Edicions 62, 1968, Vol. 1, p. 188.

IV. PORTRAITS OF HOLY WOMEN

The resolute defence of women that is articulated in the *Vita Christi* stands out in sharp contrast against the background of late-medieval Catalan literature; it has sometimes been suggested that this fact itself might allow us to read the work as a conscious contribution, on the part of Sor Isabel, to the long-running feminism/antifeminism debate which had been a recurrent feature of European culture for centuries, and which had elicited other contributions from authors as illustrious as Giovanni Boccaccio and Geoffrey Chaucer. It has often been speculated that she might have felt the need to respond, in her own fashion, to the circulation of the powerfully misogynist poem called *Espill* (or 'Mirror', written in around 1460), composed by the Valencian Jaume Roig, of which she must certainly have been aware; no direct textual connection or verbal trace, however, can establish a firm link between the two works.[9] Excessive insistence on a possible polemical engagement with this secular tradition on Sor Isabel's part might distract us from the fact that her work is above all a major piece of spiritual literature: what she undertakes in the *Vita Christi* is nothing less than a creative re-telling of the life of Jesus Christ, a literary reworking of the fundamental story in Western culture. This in itself would not have seemed a transgressive or revolutionary gesture within fifteenth-century culture, and still less in the monastic setting within which the work was produced; other such *vitae* circulated in Sor Isabel's immediate context, and her own stylistic innovations, remarkable and evocative as they were, would probably not have been appreciated by many of her first readers. Her more groundbreaking manoeuvres (and the ones which make her work directly relevant today) concern her reconstruction of the female characters that surrounded Christ according to the Gospels: an imaginative re-reading of these figures in which—while taking the traditional approach thereto as a starting-point—she manages to imagine and construct them anew. Her work amounts to nothing less than a pronounced revision of sacred history, which aims to place female dignity and the female perspective at its heart.

[9] See, for instance, the major critical article by Joan Fuster, *op. cit.*; there have also been attempts to locate the *Vita Christi* within the context of proto-feminist writing by women in a secular context: see Rosanna Cantavella, 'Isabel de Villena, la nostra Christine de Pizan', *Encontre* 2 (Winter-Spring 1986), pp. 79-86.

The figure of the Virgin Mary, of course, plays a fundamental part in Sor Isabel's approach. First and foremost, the text is not only, as its title states, a Life of Christ; it is also a *Vita Mariae*, marked in its very structure by her own life: it begins with the annunciation of her conception to her father Joachim and it closes with her death, in such a way that the very limits of the text are established by her biography. Accordingly, the existence of the Son is embedded within that of the mother, at a textual as well as a theological level: in this text, it is by first knowing and understanding her that we may come to know and understand him. The textual embedding of the Son's life within that of his mother's is, in fact, a narrative *translatio* of the continuity that exists between their bodies at a physical level. Mary is identified from the start as the *templum Dei*: it is in and through her flesh that the process of humankind's redemption is set in motion, and accordingly that flesh is presented as being without blemish or sin: she is, as the second chapter specifies, the 'immaculate conception' (a Marian tradition openly defended by Sor Isabel, even though in the fifteenth century it had not yet acquired the status of dogma within Catholic doctrine). This link of the flesh also takes the form of an experiential link: just as Mary is physically involved in the incarnational process, so she is able to experience it in greater depth than any other human being; the joys and sufferings present in her relation to Christ can thus become the most valid *figura*, or model, for that of all other souls at prayer. And, as a result, the *Vita Christi* adopts her viewpoint and follows it closely: it is through her eyes that we witness the games and playful activities of Christ as a child, that we witness his youth and his entry into public life, and quite logically the process of his Passion, death and Resurrection.

The presence of the mother is thus projected onto the very process of redemption, in such a way that this presence comes to preside over the key moments of the development whereby Christ (the human aspect of the Trinity) comes to fulfil his function in history. She is, of course, witness to the first word spoken by her son, and that word is none other than 'mother'; the word 'father', addressed to Joseph, comes only afterwards. That scene (developed between chapters LXXXIX and XC) is in itself another of the richly imagined domestic vignettes at which Sor Isabel's art excels. It begins with a depiction of the close intimacy between mother and baby, supplementing this with the aid of biblical typology (which links the first words of Christ to those of the lover in the Song of Solomon) and progresses towards the inclusion of Joseph in the scene, culminating in his celebration of the manifestation of divine love, a celebration expressed using the exclamatory language and the insistence upon an excess of grace so typical of the *Vita* ('O infinite goodness! How pleasing it is, that I should hear from Your Majesty such a charming word!'). The text thus moves from the first words of Jesus as an infant to the recognition therein of the Word itself, firmly rooting the discovery of the sublime within the realm of the homely and the domestic. The beginnings of the apostolic life of Christ, however, are also overseen by Mary, who is given a key role in responding to his initial ventures and in constituting his first audience and closest companion. A typical instance of this is provided by Sor Isabel's re-evocation of the Holy Family's sojourn in Egypt, during their exile (Chapter XCII); the stylistic strategy at work there is oriented towards the creation of an atmosphere that is humble and lowly, but which contains within it a strong sense of transcendent depths. The bodies of mother and son are brought to the forefront of the scene when Mary embraces the latter as he arrives home, carrying firewood and water, the physicality of that scene being explored in detail, even down to that detail of her hand wiping 'the little beads of sweat from his brow'. What is achieved is a close proximity, a confrontation with material existence that allows for realistic detail. From the very outset, Mary's response to her son's efforts is to share in, to feel within herself the effects of his suffering as well as participating in them ('O my Life, do you wish to exhaust yourself like this at such a young age? O my Lord and son, how *your* efforts tire *me* out!'), thus emphasising her future role as the representative of the whole of humanity, at the foot of the cross; in his response to her (here, in a direct quotation from the Latin Vulgate, anticipating quite literally the words of Paul in Corinthians 11:19), he foresees the suffering of those who will recognise and follow him. Mary is thus presented as a key influence on the development of the young Christ, at the very start of his redemptive mission: she presides over his relation to language and over his first gestures of public activity and compassion, and both aspects are presented as stemming from her nurturing, life-giving nature. The *Vita Christi* is a text in which, through the character of Mary, the female viewpoint and female flesh are placed at the origins of the drama of redemption, and are presented together as forming the key matrix from which both sacred history (i.e. the life of the historical Christ) and the literary text (i.e. the text of the *Vita* itself) may originate and develop.

To accept the existence of a basic gender difference inevitably implies, in late-medieval discourse, the assumption that intellectual and political life are the prerogative of men, yet the *Vita Christi* certainly does not build an overtly political discourse against patriarchy; what it does, however, is to recognise the position of women as the victims and the suffering subjects of history, relegated by the militaristic and power-hungry drives of men, and it consequently reaffirms the superior capacity of the former within the fields it puts forward as being transcendent: the realms of charity and love. It is perfectly possible to see enacted here one of the fundamental paradoxes of Christianity, and one which had been elaborated extensively by the Franciscan tradition: the exaltation of the humble and the lowly above the powers of the earth. In the face of all worldly authorities and value systems, the achievement of spiritual dignity is attained through a series of conceptual inversions that do not make sense in a worldly setting, but only in the eyes of God, by whom the poor are inherently preferred to the rich, the dispossessed to the mighty. So it is with women: if their lives have historically been restricted to spaces of domesticity and passivity, if they have been forced to assume the role of victims, this is only a mark of their superior dignity: their suffering and enforced submission are in themselves marks of their perseverance in Christian practice, and bring about their exaltation in the eyes of God.

A case in point is furnished by the example of the Canaanite woman who seeks the help of Jesus on behalf of her sick daughter: in Sor Isabel's re-evocation (Chapters CXXV and CXXVI), this episode in itself represents a vindication of the dignity that is achieved through humility, and through the strenuous practice of a kind of patience that takes the specific form of perseverance. The virtue of *patientia* had been traditionally understood, since the early Church Fathers, as the capacity to withstand adversity and to conform one's will to the will of God: Chapter 18 of Lactantius's *Ordinances*, for instance, glosses this theme at length, placing great emphasis upon the scant value the world will frequently attribute to the good Christian, who endures suffering quietly 'so that he will be despised as sluggish'.[10] In the *Vita Christi*, however, *patientia* is carefully distinguished from passivity: the Canaanite woman begins by basing her address to Christ upon her status as a mother ('she emerged from my innards, and there do I feel the sharp

---

[10] Lactantius, 'The Ordinances' in *The Ante-Nicene Fathers*, ed. and trans. Alexander Roberts and James Donaldson, Buffalo, Christian Literature Publishing Co., 1885, Vol. 7, p. 185.

pain of her suffering'), and upon the bodily continuity between her and her daughter; she then continues by searching through various metaphors which might allow her to describe her pain, but is forced to have recourse to the *topos* of inexpressibility ('I find no suitable name by which to call the cruel illness and affliction of my dear daughter!'). Christ enters an adjoining house and asks for its door to be shut in order to keep her away, in the knowledge that this will only lead her pleas to become more resolute and constant, and this of course is what immediately happens: her utterances become all the more expressive and urgent, being filled with direct addresses to Christ (e.g. 'look at me', 'set me free', 'open this door') which punctuate the long sentences she articulates. Most of these are structured according to a seemingly simple rhetorical format, wherein clause after clause is linked together in an ongoing paratactic flow ('and thus I shall never leave [...] and I shall ask constantly until you see fit [...] and I shall not refrain from seeking your mercy [...]'), which brings out even more clearly the anxiety of the speaker. This does not imply, of course, that Sor Isabel's style falls into a schematic pattern: on the contrary, it grows in intensity through a sustained use of accumulation (*copia*) and a constant integration of biblical quotations, which emphasise the continuity between the promises of the Old Testament and their fulfilment in Christ: ancient appeals to God once voiced in Isaiah and the Psalms have been answered now that Christ has 'decided to come down to earth clad in our own flesh'. The culmination of her address comes with her final assumption of *humilitas* via an image which she cleverly adapts from Christ's own teaching ('the whelps eat and survive on the crumbs that fall from their masters' table, and if I am not deserving of an entire loaf as a daughter, let me have a single crumb as a whelp'). It is only then that he, 'who sincerely loves the humble' responds generously to her appeal and grants her wish: he knew from the very beginning what she would say, of course, and has given her the opportunity to speak openly and publicly. The strength apparent in the voice of this woman has been shaped by its particular integration of *patientia* and *humilitas*, characteristics she has exhibited to extraordinary rhetorical effect in front of all her listeners (not to mention, readers): both qualities are deeply rooted in her experience as a mother and a woman, and both of them have had, paradoxically, an empowering quality for her, making her capable of giving verbal expression to her suffering and of achieving her purpose with Christ's blessing.

By establishing the life of the body as a privileged realm for the development of *affectus* in her female characters, the *Vita Christi* also situates that life as the essential starting-point for their proximity to Christ; in certain cases, this outlook entails a powerful subversion of the received connotations the exegetical tradition had ascribed to these figures. Sor Isabel's attention to the character of Mary Magdalene (especially in Chapters CXVIII to CXXII) can be taken to be paradigmatic of this tendency, revealing the extent to which her strategy can bring about a powerful act of re-reading and re-interpretation. Sor Isabel begins deceptively, by initially seeming to confirm the Magdalene's place within the misogynist tradition, situating her in a position which might justify the negative connotations that centuries of biblical commentary had attributed to her. To begin with, she is presented as a 'great lady', a representative member of aristocratic society and inheritor of a position of wealth (i.e. 'free from the governance of her father and mother'), circumstances which might free her from the servitude attaching to her gender. She is then set firmly within the world of fashion and dress (i.e. 'this lady loved to hold festivities and to devise outfits'), as the teacher and leader of a community of women who gather in her home (i.e. 'she had a large hall and a salon in her house where all the young ladies intent on pleasure and enjoyment would congregate'), having been attracted by her capacities as a clothes designer. Such a strong link to the world of fashion and of courtly pleasures presents her character not in terms of biblical exegesis, but rather in terms that would make it recognisable to a fifteenth-century audience: a figure who could easily be identified with some of the sophisticated courtly women that Isabel herself might have known as a child, at the Court of Maria of Aragon.

And yet it is true that her relation to the world works in an eminently sensual and aesthetic manner: in her attention to her own body, in her knowledge and practice of worldly fashion, she seems to be wholly typical of the attitudes which the misogynist tradition had identified as being essentially feminine. In this way, when her conversion occurs, what is achieved is a twofold effect. On the one hand, her transition from the physical to the spiritual is sudden and dramatic, since it takes her from the sphere of sensuality to the experience of contemplation and understanding of Christ. But on the other hand, and even more remarkably, her new proximity to Christ is also established through her bodily gestures, in a physical recognition of his presence that reinterprets her inherent sensuality and gives it a renewed transcendence. She bathes his feet with her tears and she dries them with her hair, repeating this action again and again in an 'amorous exercise'; she finally takes the liquor which she was accustomed to applying to her own body and, in a gesture of renunciation, applies it to his feet:

> So, opening a container she had brought with her, made from a very unique kind of stone, within which there sat a costly oil that she was in the habit of using to preserve her delicate body, and deciding to bring to an end such pleasures and delights and to put everything to use in the service of her beloved, she poured the said oil, thereby anointing and refreshing the tired feet of Our Lord, and considered it to be very well invested in the service of the Creator of all things, who in such hardship and need had trudged across this wretched world for the sake of the salvation of sinners (p. 106).

The 'pleasures and delights' which characterised her previous existence are reinterpreted and transformed and, in the process, they acquire a new dignity. The gesture itself is slowly and elegantly described; from her initial care for the body, Mary Magdalene moves towards the care of the soul through her new relationship to Christ; but this movement may itself be expressed physically and sensually, since her physicality and sensuality have received new meaning. Mary Magdalene's attention to her own body, or her awareness of her own sensuality, has been transformed and reinterpreted positively: it has become a variety of the capacity for *affectus* that characterises the female condition as a whole. In the work of Isabel de Villena, the holiness of women stems primarily from their very femininity: their voices, gestures and bodies are already disposed, because of their nature, towards a privileged encounter with the sacred.

Sor Isabel's response to the misogynist tradition, then, is not articulated simply as a polemical counter-attack, or as a mere affirmation of female virtues through the accumulation of illustrious *exempla*. Her general strategy is more subtle, as well as more effective in rhetorical terms. The text of the *Vita Christi* tends to accept traditional forms of gender differentiation and to acknowledge the association of femaleness with matter and sensuality rather than with abstract thought and form; it tends to present affective life, and the awareness of the body, as essentially feminine traits. To that extent, a part of its argumentation would seem to play into the hands of the polarisation between the masculine and the feminine that had justified the intellectual and physical subjugation of women from the days of the Church Fathers until the late-Middle Ages. But on the other hand, and systematically throughout the text, the dominant interpretation of that polarisation is turned on its head: it is the conceptual association of woman with materiality and with emotion which is presented as the basis for their superior capacity for love and charity. The *Vita Christi*, as a whole, shows no trace of the Platonic mistrust of sensuality, of the flesh and of the senses, as well as of the superficiality of representations; on the contrary, because of its debt to the tradition of affective spirituality, it acknowledges the importance of the senses and of the experience of material reality in the creation of subjectivity. Mothering, nurturing, feeding: all of these bodily experiences are quintessentially female, as are the supervision of the family, the administration of food, the care over other bodies and their needs; even the sensual attention to one's own body (dramatised in the case of Mary Magdalene) is no more than a deformed version of the female awareness of the conditioning of the flesh, of women's attention to the physical particularities of life. To the extent that women are primary and conscious participants in the realities of material existence, they are also more naturally attuned to compassion, more capable of becoming solid, dignified models of morality and love.

Theological discourse and the exploration of the emotions thus complement each other throughout the text of the *Vita Christi*: the constant use of biblical quotation, and the interpolation of brief commentaries thereon, keep the text firmly within the bounds of orthodoxy and give it a stable doctrinal grounding. In this way, Isabel de Villena manages to deliver one of the more remarkable defences of female dignity in late-medieval culture, and one that is as striking and significant in its way as the *De Claris Mulieribus* or as *La Cité des Dames*, even while adopting a very different framework from the humanistic model used by Boccaccio or Christine de Pizan: one in which biblical commentary both facilitates and authorises a full and resolute reappraisal of womanhood.

V. A CASE STUDY: RE-READING EVE (*VITA CHRISTI* CXCVII)

To inscribe female experience and the female body at the centre of human history necessarily implied, for a late-medieval writer, a confrontation with sin, the basic spiritual factor that, according to the Christian world-view, conditioned all human existence. Sor Isabel achieves an audacious perspective when considering the latter subject, and formulates an approach towards it that involves a strong revisionist effort, one which also has remarkable consequences in terms of gender. This is carried out through a powerful re-evaluation of the figure of Eve, a figure who in the *Vita Christi* is viewed as being far more than the traditional counterpart of Mary: through a powerful inversion (which nevertheless manages to remain, as we shall see, within the limits of Catholic orthodoxy), Eve is perceived not merely as the origin of perdition but as that of the entire progress of humanity and its transcendent history. Of course the character of Eve had lain, for several centuries, at the heart of a complex web of discussions and theological exegesis, these being consistently oriented towards a misogynist perspective: that tradition had tended to represent her, since the early days of the Church Fathers, as a fundamental example of human weakness and of the innate female disposition towards sin. Let us appreciate for a moment the accusatory heft of this *locus classicus* in one of its oldest formulations, namely, a fragment from the treatise *De cultu feminarum* by Tertullian (end of the second century AD):

> You are the devil's gateway, you are the unsealer of that forbidden tree: you are the first deserter of the divine law: you are she who persuaded him whom the devil was not valiant enough to attack. You destroyed so easily God's image, man. And on account of your desert, death, even the Son of God had to die.[11]

The inculpatory force of this passage is not diminished, but rather increased by the fact that its implicit addresee, the 'you' to whom Tertullian speaks, is not Eve herself but actually any woman: for the apologist Father, all of them could be identified with their original mother, and therefore accused of her same weakness and propensity to moral error. The second book of Genesis narrates the seduction of Eve by Satan and the successive introduction of sin into the world through the former's offer of the forbidden fruit to Adam: that text had repeatedly been interpreted within the patristic tradition as indicating the intrinsic weakness of woman, who had been tempted first because of her greater vulnerability. Let us observe, for instance, how that original myth was explained by Augustine of Hippo in *De civitate Dei* (early-fifth century AD):

[11] Tertullian, 'On the Apparel of Women', in *The Ante-Nicene Fathers, op. cit.,* Vol. 4, p. 14.

> [The serpent] had deceitful conversation with the woman, no doubt start-
> ing with the inferior of the human pair so as to arrive at the whole by stages, sup-
> posing that the man would not be so easily gullible, and could not be trapped by
> a false move on his own part, but only if he yielded to another's mistake [...]. We
> cannot believe that man was led astray to transgress God's law because he believed
> that the woman spoke the truth, but that he fell in with her suggestions because
> they were as closely bound in partnership [...]. Hence the Apostle does not say,
> 'He did not sin', but 'He was not seduced'.[12]

Such a distinction between the respective male and the female dis-
positions towards sin also implied a difference between the corresponding capacities of men and women, and this would lead in time to a different moral gradation of the natural tendencies of both genders. A central emphasis would be put by the exegetical tradition on the fact that,
while men and women were equally endowed with an *anima rationalis*,
and therefore were jointly set above all other beings in the order of creation, women had a stronger tendency to be dominated by the demands
of the *anima sensitiva*, and therefore were less capable of abstract thought,
and in need of moral and spiritual guidance on the part of men.

We have already seen how the *Vita Christi* works towards a defence of
the dignity of women by reinterpreting the significance of the characteristics that had been traditionally ascribed to the female sex. To the extent
that the life of Christ has universal significance, it must be read in terms of
the whole history of humanity, and thereby compensate for the introduction of sin into the world by Adam and Eve; and it is in relation to the drama
of redemption that the character and voice of Eve are brought into the
Vita. Sor Isabel presents the culminating scene of the crucifixion as being
fully endowed with redemptive significance, the death of Christ therein
bringing about a reconciliation between God and humanity; it is in the
chapters that follow this transcendental moment, namely, in the interval
between his death and his resurrection (CLXXXVI to CCVI) that he finally
encounters the founding fathers of humanity, spending time in the company of the major figures of Israelite and pre-Christian history. And it is at
that point (Chapter CXCVII) that the voice of Eve herself is heard. She
begins by placing a strong emphasis on the significance of original sin,
which is read here (quite logically in a work that places such great stress
upon the role of *humilitas*) as an act of pride: she remembers her desire

---

[12] Augustine of Hippo, *The City of God*, trans. Henry Bettenson and introd. John
O'Meara, London, Penguin Books, 1984, p. 570.

'to know all things' and the fact that such a desire led to the corruption of 'all human nature'; she relentlessly attributes to herself all responsibility for the introduction of suffering into the world (i.e. 'my fault'); importantly, the character of Adam is left very much in the background, featuring almost as a passive participant in the original sin. Also from the very outset, however, her language is entirely permeated by the expression of a penitential attitude: stylistically, through the use of exclamatory and vocative sequences (e.g. 'O my Lord and my God!', 'O Lord') and the use of adjectives and prepositional clauses that underscore constantly her excess of pain (e.g. 'pierced through with sorrow', 'excess of sorrow'): the word *dolor* (i.e. 'sorrow') is, in fact, a pervasive presence throughout the text, a word which in the original Catalan appears in constant variations: as a noun, an adjective and a verb. The notion of suffering is expressed here cumulatively, as the various stages of Eve's self-imposed penance are explained. For she represents herself here as submitting to a series of purgative processes, some of which would be familiar to the conventual audience of the *Vita*: first, via the mortification of her flesh (e.g. 'I humbled my heart […] I cast myself to the ground'); second, via her practice of fasting (e.g. 'grasses and water alone were my sustenance'); and, third, via her self-willed isolation and seclusion (e.g. 'for a hundred years was I shut away within a cave cut off from the company of Adam […]'). All of this amounts to a preliminary move towards her re-interpretation as a character: from being the original sinner, the 'devil's gateway', Eve here becomes the paradigm of a penitential attitude.

In response to Eve's suffering voice, it is Christ himself who speaks, completing the re-interpretation of her figure and projecting it towards a theological level. In another of the radical emotional and conceptual transitions characteristic of the *Vita*, he invites her to transform her sorrow into joy and to move from her deep awareness of sin into a proportional position of honour: her role is to be celebrated rather than lamented, and she is to be held in reverence as befits her place in history. After all, it was on account of her sin that the entire machinery of redemption was made necessary, and it must thus be read as the ultimate cause of the joy that Christ will bring to humanity. We are entering here a very specific theological domain: the concept of *felix culpa* or 'Fortunate Fall', which had been repeatedly explored as a major form of theodicy since at least Saint Augustine, and which had acquired considerable strength within the soteriological discourse of the late-medieval Church. This theory had presented the Fall itself as a

necessary though painful step in the development of humanity: sin and
death had certainly been allowed to enter the world, but this in itself
had laid the groundwork for raising that world to a much higher position than it had enjoyed in Eden. This paradox had received its clear-
est formulation in the following words attributed to Saint Augustine:
'O quam feliciter cecedi, qui post lapsum felicius resurrexi!' ('O how
fortunately did I fall who am more fortunately resurrected after the
fault');[13] the presence of sin has made the processes of the Incarnation
and Redemption necessary, and by participating therein humanity is
able to enter into a closer, and more perfect knowledge of God than it
originally had. In the *Vita Christi*, Eve is recognised as being the principal agent who has made such a historical progression possible. Her role
in history, rather than being one of corruption and deprivation, has
been an *enabling* one, the starting point in humanity's progress towards
complete proximity to God:

> Now begins your happiness and joy, which shall have no end; your sin has now
> been pardoned and forgiven. Henceforth you shall speak to your daughters, here
> present, only of delights and pleasures, in the awareness that you are all so beloved
> and glorified by me. Great has been your sin, and a great redeemer have you
> deserved by means of your wholesome repentance. And if you have caused great
> harm to the world by your sin, I have made it all the more beautiful and all the more
> noble by my suffering and death, and those who are saved after that sin shall have
> all the more glory on account of the worthiness of my suffering, upon which shall
> be founded all the endeavours of the elect. And by this example of my death many
> shall accept martyrdom and shall achieve outstanding levels of glory; not only
> men, but also women... (p. 141).

To situate Eve as the starting-point in humanity's progress towards
God entails a radical reformulation of the misogynist discourse in her
regard; it also, and necessarily, begins to dismantle the well-established
polar opposition between her and the Virgin Mary. The voice of Christ
does not dwell on the traditional contrasts between Eve and Mary
(damnation vs redemption, pride vs humility, sensuality vs spirituality);
on the contrary, it deliberately undermines and suppresses them, while
on the other hand it asserts the similarities between both figures: one
has engendered humanity, the other has engendered its Saviour; one is

---

[13] The passage appears in the treatise *De diligendo Deo*, one of the works of uncertain authorship which have been repeatedly attributed to Augustine; see Augustine of
Hippo, *Opera omnia*, Paris, 1841, Vol. 6, p. 6.

the mother of all men, the other is the mother of God in his human form. Such similarity is rooted in the fundamental and common feature they share, namely, the fact that it has been in their bodies, and through the agency of their will, that the history of humanity and of its salvation has been made possible. The two of them are to be seen as jointly commanding respect and worship, because it is through their complementary actions that the universal process of salvation has taken place: Eve has situated humanity as the subject of history, and Mary has contributed towards bringing about its redemption and its joyful progress towards glory. Finally, and in an even more transgressive turn, to Eve is assigned a new function: that of universal intercessor for humanity before God, and on behalf of women in particular; her central position as the origin and material source of history establishes her as a beneficial presence, presiding over the progress of her gender throughout the whole of history:

> And I wish you [i.e. Eve] to be held in great reverence and devotion by men and women, as the unique mother of all, and for you continually to act on their behalf as intercessor in my presence, and particularly on behalf of women, on whom I shall bestow innumerable graces, out of love for you, if I learn that they hold you in singular devotion and reverence. For I have instructed those to honour their mother who wish to live long in the love of my grace; and through Solomon have I said: '*Generatio quae matrem suam non benedicit non est lota sordibus*', for children who do not honour their mother cannot be free from great blame (pp. 141-142).

This does not come in spite of Eve's position as representative of her sex, but precisely *as a consequence* of that representative role: the female body, symbolised in the image of the original mother, is firmly acknowledged as being essentially creative and life-giving, as the site which has made life possible and in which it is constantly regenerated in physical and spiritual terms. One of the crucial features of the misogynist tradition has been confronted head-on and, in a bold revisionist move, it has been dismantled from within and rendered inert.

If the *Vita Christi* continues to speak to us today, if it continues to be relevant five centuries after its first printing, it is because it deliberately places the female body and female experience at the centre of history and of human experience. Firmly rooted as it is in the meditative and exegetical traditions of its day, it gestures towards modernity in inviting us to re-evaluate the text of the Bible and to interpret it anew, by retrieving the women's voices that speak within it, re-creating them imaginatively and endowing them with a full sense of dignity: a lesson still valid for gender studies and for feminist theology today, and one whose relevance is only likely to increase over time.

Joan Curbet

Translator's Preface

THIS TRANSLATION is based on Albert-Guillem Haufi Valls' select edition of Isabel de Villena's *Vita Christi* (Barcelona, Edicions 62, 1995). On occasion I have had reason to consult a recent French translation by Patrick Gifreu (2008), one based upon a different edition of the text (see Cantavella & Parra [1987]), which nevertheless covers similar ground to the present selection of chapters, though for editorial reasons, is in dramatically condensed form.

Owing to the frequency of biblical quotations in Villena's work, I have had recourse to the Latin Vulgate, The Douay-Rheims Bible (Challoner Version) and the Revised Standard Version. Catholic Edition, not to mention the King James Bible for possible guidance when translating the translations and glosses which follow such passages in the *Vita Christi*. All biblical references and conflated quotations from different biblical books appear in the notes. Similarly, I have tried to reference as many of the non-biblical quotations which occur throughout the text as possible; such references are also included in the footnotes. The references given to non-biblical authors, however, are not intended to give the impression that Sor Isabel had direct recourse to the works cited; merely to suggest that she may have come to know parts of them through the medium of various florilegia or other intermediate sources. Many of Sor Isabel's putative sources are freely available on the Internet, and a good number of them can be consulted (in context) in the relevant volumes of J.-P. Migne's *Patrologia Latina. Cursus Completus* (PL). In certain cases I have consulted the holdings of the British Library.

I have at all times attempted to bear witness to the characteristic style and lexical features of Isabel de Villena's *Vita Christi*. Hers is a style which is very often direct, expostulatory, dialogic, optative and, at times, exhortative. In lexical terms, however, as a result of the reduced palette and insistent repetitiveness of Sor Isabel's choice of vocabulary, particularly when focusing on her protagonists' emotional responses (e.g. pronounced joy or sorrow at the events narrated), and the corresponding narrowness of appropriate English language terms to describe such feelings, the modern-day translator is faced with a dilemma. Should he or she preserve the cumulative persistence of such terms, often densely spread throughout relatively compact sections of the text (here presumably such aggregations serving to reinforce the meditative functions of the work) or should he or she introduce an element of variation therein, more in line with the expectations of a contemporary readership (more demanding and sophisticated in terms of lexical richness, perhaps, than Isabel de Villena's intended audience, namely, her fellow sisters at the Convent of the Holy Trinity, though less sophisticated in terms of familiarity with biblical and profane authors)? In the event, I have chosen to dilute wherever possible the greatest concentrations of such repeated or homologous terms, while retaining their general affective content and overall mood. A similar dilemma arises in the case of the author's recurrent usage of epithets such as the Catalan *excel·lent* and *singular* which cannot always be translated in a literal manner. I have adopted an analogous procedure in cases such as these.[14] Likewise, the omnipresent adjective *gran* ('great') and the expression *ab molt de…* ('with much…'), have often necessitated a fuller, adverbial treatment in English (e.g. deep/deeply, warm/warmly, full/fully or similar alternatives).

I have also 'Anglicised' certain honorific titles assigned to Jesus, the Blessed Virgin, and Mary Magdalene, in such a way that *lo Senyor* and *la Senyora* are familiarised, to read 'Our Lord' and 'Our Lady' (including the coinages 'Our Excellent Lady', and even 'Our Excellent Magdalene'). Similarly, other honorific titles for personages, which are either untranslatable or would excessively weigh down an English text, have been suppressed, even while preserving Sor Isabel de Villena's affection for the correct terms of courtly address, a register into which much of her *Vita Christi* has been cast.

As regards the question of Sor Isabel's 'feminine style', I have simply attempted to stick as closely to the text she produced as possible; in this, I trust I have been sensitive to the major aspects of that style. Although both

[14] Particular instances of both can be found in Chapters IV, LXI, LXXXIX, and CXXV, to mention but a few.

men and women are bound by the same set of grammatical rules in a given language, as a male translator, however, of a work by a woman (and a fifteenth-century nun at that) my specific decisions, lexical, syntactical and otherwise, could not avoid being those of a man; nevertheless, they are those of a man cognisant of the fact that he is translating the work of a woman.

I should like to thank Dr Joan Santanach, my editor at Barcino, for his customary helpfulness, as well as Dr Joan Curbet of the Universitat Autònoma de Barcelona for commissioning me to undertake this translation, not to mention the publisher's reader, Francesc J. Gómez also of the Universitat Autònoma de Barcelona, for reading my final version of the text.

Robert D. Hughes
Prague and Sedlejovice, July 2012

PORTRAITS OF HOLY WOMEN

Preface

THE RESPLENDENT LIGHT of devotion that shines within Your Highness has revealed to you that in this your monastery a devout *Vita Christi* had been set in order by the illustrious Lady Elionor, otherwise known as Sister Isabel de Villena, our Reverend Abbess and our Mother; and because Your Royal Excellency, wholly inflamed with love of the great King of Paradise, had written to ask the General Bailiff of this your kingdom of Valencia to send you a copy of that work, I intend to perform this welcome service for Your Majesty, so that it might reach your royal hands sooner, by having that work printed.

And because, in the deep and woeful vale of tears that is this wretched world, those who rise on the wings of some worldly praise descend further into the innermost depths of tormenting Hell, while those who make their way along the lowly paths of simple humility draw nearer to the summit of the City of Paradise, the virtuous and most honourable Mother Abbess, my predecessor, considering by the light of her clear understanding the dangers that worldly praise brings, had descended to such innermost depths of humility that she did not wish to write her name in any part of this book, fearing that her virtuous deeds, shut away within the archives of humility, might come under assault from the iniquitous hands of vainglory. So, ablaze in her the ignited torches of the luminosity residing in her most illustrious stock, just as her royal kinsfolk[1] had sown innumerable acts of glorious repute through their exaltation of the holy Christian faith, she, most devout mother, has sought to sow upon the white paper of this book the seed of her purified conscience, that those who read it may reap the fruits of profitable teachings; entreating the great king Jesus to be the sailor and pilot of the boat of her understanding so that she might safely sail in the vast sea of his blessed life. And the rays of the bright sun of justice, entering through the windows of her shining intellect, thus inflamed it with ardent charity, so that it might seek through laborious efforts to compose such an immense volume and book as this.

And since she, a humble nun, is praised for having kept her name silent when composing such a worthy book, I believe myself, as a result, to achieve no small merit before God by divulging the name of such a singular Mother, worthy as she is of immortal memory: Sister Isabel de Villena wrote it; Sister Isabel de Villena composed it; Sister Isabel de Villena, in an elegant and gentle style, lent order to it, not only for the devout sisters and the daughters of obedience who inhabit the closed house of this monastery, but also for all those who live during this brief, irksome and transitory life.

I, a most serene and Christian lady, send it to Your Highness. Herein shall you find such profound and lofty thoughts that you will plainly admit that the Holy Spirit guided the understanding and the quill of a Mother so honourable and reverend, who was so devoted to the service of Your Excellency, the life and estate of whom may the Most Holy Trinity exalt and cause to prosper.

From your city of Valencia, on the twenty-ninth day of the month of March, in the year 1497.

The humble servant and supplicant of Your Royal Highness, Sister Aldonça de Montsoriu, unworthy Abbess of the Monastery of the Holy Trinity.

---

[1] See Introduction for details of the Lady Elionor's noble birth and adoption of the name Isabel on entry to her convent.

HERE BEGINS A *VITA CHRISTI* IN ROMANCE,[1]
SO THAT SIMPLE AND IGNORANT FOLK MIGHT HAVE KNOWLEDGE OF
AND CONTEMPLATE THE LIFE AND DEATH OF OUR REDEEMER AND LORD, JESUS,
WHO LOVES US, AND TO WHOM SHOULD BE GIVEN GLORY AND HONOUR FOR ALL OUR
DEEDS, AS THE ONE WHO PERFORMS
AND ORDAINS THEM

---

[1] Meaning the Catalan vernacular.

Part One: Mary and the Holy Family

ON HOW THE MOST CHASTE CONCEPTION OF HIS MOST HOLY DAUGHTER WAS PROCLAIMED TO SAINT JOACHIM BY AN ANGEL

I

ECCE IAM VENIT plenitudo temporis.[1] Since the fullness of time ordained by Our Lord God was approaching and drawing near, in which His Majesty had decided to apply himself to the reparation and salvation of human nature, and because, in order to perform such a lofty undertaking, it was necessary for him to come down to the world of captivity, where the wretched sons of Adam were exiled, and he knew full well that in the whole of the said world there was not a decent home within which he might rest, it therefore pleased him to command and ordain that an abode be built such as pertained to His Majesty, one wrought with such excellent and singular workmanship that its like had never been devised, insofar as those who saw it should be bound to say, in admiration of the beauty of this house: '*Non est hic aliud nisi domus Dei et porta caeli*',[2] meaning, 'This abode has undoubtedly been built and constructed for His Majesty Our Lord God alone, and nobody else should stay in it. And by means of this most sacred abode shall a ladder be found to ascend to the heights of the Kingdom of Paradise, unknown to and unseen by men.'

[1] Cf. Galatians 4:4; for the precise wording of this opening sentence, see R. J. Hesbert, *Corpus antiphonalium officii*, 6 vols., Rome, 1963-1979, no. 6596.
[2] Genesis 28:17.

So, in order to bring the said house to completion, His Divine Majesty ordered a great prince of angels, his Royal Master of Lodgings, to be summoned, and said to him: 'Go, Master of Lodgings, *in vallem lacrimarum*,[3] and seek a great builder, unknown to and unloved by men, but rather cast out and scorned as a sterile man, who is named Joachim, and is greatly beloved by me, and whom I have set aside for this singular task of building my abode. And tell him on my behalf that, together with his most holy wife Anne, they are to construct my house, in which I particularly wish to lay the first foundation stone.'

The Master of Lodgings, having been informed at length about the magnificence and beauty of the house which Our Lord had ordered to be built, left that place without delay in order to deal swiftly with his embassy. But when he had arrived on earth, he found there nothing but *labor et dolor*,[4] for everybody was engaged in a multitude of toil and suffering beyond description. Feeling deep compassion for those captive people, he looked among them for the builder he sought, finding him in the rugged mountains, with the shepherds of his flock, with whom he was discussing his anguish and distress, since he had thus been cast out of the temple on account of his sterility, for which he no longer had hopes of a remedy. As a result, he had decided to end his life in that solitude, away from his wife Anne and from all his kinsfolk and friends. The simple shepherds had helped to sympathise with the anguish of their master.

The prince of angels, who had come in human form, approached them and, greeting Joachim, said to him: '*Qui sunt hii sermones quos confertis inter vos et estis tristes?*',[5] meaning: 'O Lord Joachim, what are the deeply distressing reasons of which you speak, and which bring such sadness to your features, as to those of your loyal shepherds who take your suffering as their own?'

Joachim, unaware that it was an angel, replied to him by saying: 'O virtuous young man, since you can tell from my demeanour that my sorrow is indescribable, why do you wish to cause me such suffering that I should have to give voice to it over and again? For I swear on my faith that each time *dolor meus renovatus est*.[6] I thus ask you, please, not to increase

---

[3] From Psalm 83 [84]:7.

[4] From Psalm 89 [90]:10.

[5] St Thomas Aquinas, *Catena aurea in quatuor evangelia. Expositio in Lucam*, Chapter 24, Lesson 2.

[6] From Psalm 38 [39]:3.

my suffering, since you are unable to reduce it. If you are so keen to hear about my anguish, *interroga eos qui audierunt me*, [7] may it please you to ask these servants of mine here present, for they have heard from me the entire reason for my suffering, which I am no longer able to recount another time.'

So the angel, wishing to reveal himself to him, said: 'O brave nobleman, who descends from that tribe of Judah, from the true royal line of the House of David, do not lose heart! *Ego sum angelus Domini, et missus sum ad te loqui*,[8] for I am the angel of Our Lord God, sent by His Majesty to utter and communicate to you the great and lofty wonders of his which he has decided to perform on earth. For he desires and commands that you, Lord Joachim, return to your wife whom with such distress you have abandoned, and who shall conceive from you a daughter of such excellence and rank, *quia nullus dicere possit aliquam ante eam similem ei fuisse nec post eam futuram*,[9] since you may be sure, Lord Joachim, that nobody can say that before this lady has there been anything like her in the entire universe, nor that after, in the future, shall anyone equal to her be found. *Haec est illa lux quam dixit Deus ut fieret, de qua factus est sol;*[10] for this is the light that Our Lord ordered to be made and from which the sun is fashioned, for Our Lord God, who is the true sun of justice, shall be born of this lady, your daughter. He has chosen her from eternity to be his temple, and of her in truth may it be said: *Hoc est templum Dei magnum et famosum, in quo malleus et ferreum non sunt audita cum aedificaretur;* for this is the holy temple of Our Lord God, great and widely renowned in terms of its construction, which means to say that, as regards her conception, His Majesty does not wish any blows of hammer or tool to be audible, for that heavy and ponderous burden of original sin in her shall not be found, nor hammer blow of any guilt on her be heard.

'For she is the imperial queen, who is not included in or comprised by any common law; but rather Our Lord God says to her: "*Non pro te, sed pro omnibus haec lex constituta est*",[11] meaning, when he speaks to that lady at

---

[7] Cf. John 18:21.

[8] Cf. Luke 1:19.

[9] Sor Isabel here echoes the allusion to Solomon in 1 Kings (Third Book of Kings) 3:12, the king who had entrusted to God the building of the temple. See Lesley K. Twomey, 'Sor Isabel de Villena: A Gendered Perspective on the Immaculate Conception', *Journal of Catalan Studies*, 2003 [http://www.anglo-catalan.org/jocs/6/articles/twomey/index.html].

[10] Cf. John 8:12.

[11] Esther 15:13 (Vulgate); 15:10 (RSV-CE).

her unprecedented conception: "Do not fear, my temple, for although you are descended from the proper nature of Adam's stock, you will not fall under the law constituted by his sin, but rather under that privileged by my grace to a singular degree. *Quia ego elegi te*,[12] for I have chosen you as my palace and resting place, and I wish you to be the garden of my delights."

'O Joachim, what can this lady lack, insofar as Our Lord God purposely wishes to create her to be his mother? For along with her rank as mother, she will achieve all the distinctions that, outside God, may be communicated to an angelic or human creature, since, when creating that glorious soul, he shall clothe it in his grace, and shall adorn it with such lofty and singular jewels, that in her shall be confirmed the saying in Ecclesiasticus: "*Ipse creavit eam in spiritu suo, vidit et dinumeravit et mensuravit*",[13] meaning: Our Lord God has created this excellent lady according to his pleasure and will, as well as to the contentment of his spirit; he has seen her for eternity and with her has he fallen in love; he alone is able to count her splendours, and to measure her loftiness and rank. *Vere templum est Spiritus Sancti, et palatium filii Dei, et sponsalis thalamus Patris aeterni*, for truly this lady is the excellent temple of the Holy Spirit, and the royal palace of the Son of God, and the grand marriage bed of the eternal Father's betrothal. To her Our Lord God said through the mouth of David: "*Elevata est magnificentia tua super caelos*",[14] meaning that His Majesty had decided to exalt and extol her above every angelic nature.

'And, as soon as her glorious soul has been created and united to her body, he intends to clothe and adorn her with his grace to a singular degree. For first of all he shall place a magnificent carbuncle[15] on her head, that is to say, Our Lady's singular and steadfast memory, wherein the eternal Father shall be lodged, revealing his infinite power in this first room so richly endowed by His Majesty.

'The second room, which is this lady's understanding, shall be of such brightness that in the dark night of this world it will light up and shine, surpassing Seraphim and Cherubim in its luminosity and loftiness of wisdom, and will contemplate more vividly the sublimity and excellence of God, and will discern in them more than would any mere creature. In this room shall the omnipotent Son of God be lodged, imprinting thereupon

[12] Haggai 2:24.
[13] Ecclesiasticus [Sirach] 1:9.
[14] An antiphon from a Gregorian chant.
[15] A red precious stone.

his divine wisdom to such an exceptional degree that he will be able to say to her: "O greatly beloved temple of mine! *Dedi tibi cor sapiens et intelligens, in tantum ut nullus ante te similis tui fuerit, nec post te surrecturus sit*",[16] the Son of God seeking to tell the newly created lady: "I have chosen you as a temple for myself, I have given you an extremely wise and highly intelligent heart and memory, in such plenty and abundance that nobody before you has been your like nor afterwards shall be."

'The third room of this house of God shall be the will of this lady, altogether roused. And here shall be lodged the Holy Spirit, presenting to her at the main entrance his seven gifts, as it is written: "*Super quam septem dona Spiritus Sancti plenissime requiescunt*", for upon this lady shall fully rest all the said seven gifts of the Holy Spirit.

'In these three most holy rooms shall abide and dwell the three divine persons, each in his own, and all three together in each. *Quia opera Trinitatis non sunt divisa.*[17]

'And, in order that this spouse of his be properly accompanied according to her estate, Our Lord God wished seven handmaids of singular distinction to be chosen from throughout his entire dominions, to serve and accompany Our Lady within the womb of her mother and throughout her entire life, so that they might be her principal maidservants most beloved by her.

'The name of the first shall be Faith; she will make her firmly believe all that is contained within the Law and the Prophets. The second shall bear the name Hope; she will make her hope with great desire to see all God's promises fulfilled. The third shall bear the name exceptional Charity; she will inflame her so greatly with the love of God and of her neighbours that she will continually labour to reconcile Our Lord God with human nature. The fourth shall be named holy Humility; she will make her know and love the singular graces bestowed upon her by Our Lord God, and, for these, render unto him continual praise and thanks. The fifth shall bear the name ardent Devotion; she will maintain within her a continuous arousal and insatiable desire to pray. The sixth shall be named Mercy; she will make her keep her heart open, to welcome the poor and succour the needy. The seventh is named Compassion; she will make her feel pity towards the afflicted and assist them promptly in their needs.

---

[16] God's words to King Solomon in 1 Kings (Third Book of Kings) 3:12.

[17] A classical formulation of Trinitarian doctrine *ad extra*.

'Behold, Lord Joachim, how His Divine Majesty wishes your daughter to be. And if any shall marvel at her great distinction, may they receive the reply: "*Dominus opus habet*", meaning: "Our eternal Lord God requires her to be thus, in order to be his mother; he has painted her and adorned her with a device in line with how he needed her to be and with what was pleasing to him".'

So, having heard these arguments, Joachim almost lost his mind, both from the most intense astonishment and from his singular joy, and was unable to speak for a long period of time. But recovering his strength, he said: '*Magnus est Deus noster super omnes deos! Quis ergo poterit praevidere ut aedificet ei dignam domum? Si caelum et caeli caelorum capere eum non queunt, quantus ego sum ut possim ei aedificare domum?*',[18] meaning: 'O angel, great is our Lord and God, and more wondrous than all the gods! Who is the one prudent and wise enough to build a house worthy of His Majesty? Neither the sky nor all the heavens is able to hold him. Who am I to build a house for him?'

The angel said in reply: 'O Lord Joachim, do you not recall the words of your ancestor David, who said: "*Nisi Dominus aedificaverit domum, in vanum laboraverunt qui aedificant eam?*"[19] For, if the Lord did not have a hand in this task, your labours would be futile and in vain, for His Majesty has said: "*Sine me nichil potestis facere.*"[20] Truly, after himself, it is you he wishes to be the builder of this house, and to obtain the glory of having built a temple of God easily more outstanding than did Solomon; and you shall have this unique prerogative among all the saints: for you shall be called the father of the Mother of God, and for this reason shall you be honoured above all men.'

When he heard this, Joachim prostrated himself on the ground and worshipped Our Lord God, thanking him for his lofty wonders by saying: 'O infinite wisdom and power without end! What is written is certainly very true: "*Quod est impossibile apud homines, hoc est possibile apud Deum*",[21] for what seemed impossible to men, namely, my having children—on account of which I have been so greatly abused and scorned, and with such great insults cast out from the temple—has, since you, Sir, have willed it, become possible and feasible. *Quia non est confusio sperantibus in te,*[22] for

---

[18] 2 Paralipomenon (2 Chronicles) 2:5-6.
[19] Psalm 126 [127]:1.
[20] John 15:5.
[21] Matthew 19:26.
[22] Daniel 3:40.

those who sincerely place their hope in you cannot stay shamed for long. My ancestor David had certainly experienced the sweetness of your mercy, when he said: "*Secundum multitudinem dolorum meorum in corde meo, consolationes tuae laetificaverunt animam meam*",[23] for, in keeping with the sufferings borne patiently by the afflicted, you, Sir, bestow upon them your consolations in much greater abundance, as I note in myself from experience; for which, Sir, I remain more grateful to you than all the men in the world, and I give you boundless thanks for this mercy shown to me and to my entire family.'

So, since the angel was preparing to depart, Joachim said to him: 'O Glorious prince, if I have found grace in your presence, please do me the honour of coming to my tent, which is very close by, and there take a light repast.'

But the angel answered him: 'Lord Joachim, I welcome and appreciate greatly your charitable urge, and give you boundless thanks for your invitation. *Quia cibus meus invisibilis est, et potus meus a nullo mortali potest videri*,[24] for my food is invisible, and my drink cannot be seen by any mortal. So, Lord Joachim, do not linger, but rather go without delay to your lady wife, who is very worried by your absence; and I shall go first to console her and tell her to come out to greet you.'

After the angel had bidden farewell, Joachim recounted the vision to his shepherds, who were very loyal to him, and they said to him: 'Sir, let us leave you immediately, and may you obey the command of Our Lord God and his angel.' And so they set off, going on foot.

---

[23] Psalm 93 [94]:19.

[24] From the probably early-seventh century apocryphal *Gospel of the Pseudo-Matthew*, 3:2 (also known as 'The Book About the Origin of the Blessed Mary and the Childhood of the Saviour'), a source of information on the early life of Christ and the life of Mary during the Middle Ages. For the parallels between the end of Joachim's dialogue with the angel and the *Gospel of the Pseudo-Matthew*, see M. de Riquer, *Història de la literatura catalana*, 4 vols., Esplugues de Llobregat, 1964, Vol. 3, pp. 461-462.

ON HOW THE SAME ANGEL REVEALED TO THE GLORIOUS
ANNE THE PRIVILEGED CONCEPTION OF HER EXCELLENT
DAUGHTER, TO WHOM SHE WOULD GIVE THE NAME MARY

II

THE ANGEL SUDDENLY appeared in Anne's house, and finding her at
prayer, very tearful and distressed, he said to her: '*Dominus misit me ad te,
quem dilexisti mente et puro corde*',[1] meaning: 'Anne, feel infinite joy, and
put a stop to your tears, for the Lord whom you love with your heart and
mind has sent me to you with the words: "*Tristitia vestra convertetur in
gaudium, et gaudium vestrum nemo tollet a vobis*",[2] for your sadness shall be
turned into singular joy, and no one shall take your joy away from you, for
be sure, Lady Anne, that Solomon has said of you: "*Invenit gratiam coram
oculis Domini*", for you have found grace in the presence of Our Lord God,
and your prayers are heard by His Majesty, and he has decided to give you
much more than you have requested, since you merely asked for a son or
daughter similar to other sinners, whereas Our Lord God wishes you to
conceive a daughter so singular that neither original, venial, nor mortal
sin shall ever be found in her. Pure of all guilt shall you conceive her, and
pure shall you raise her. And in purity and spotlessness shall her entire life
be led, for Our Lord God has said of this lady, through the mouth of
Solomon: "*Pulchra es, amica mea, et macula non est in te.*"[3]

[1] Text from a Gregorian chant generally sung on the Feast of St Agatha, Virgin and
Martyr, 5th February (specifically during Matins, Nocturn 1, Responsory 3).
[2] A conflation of John 16:20 and 16:22.
[3] Song of Solomon 4:7.

'You, Lady Anne, wish to multiply your people; this excellent daughter of yours shall be the lantern which brings divine light in order to save everyone in the world; yet no one shall perish other than through his own fault. You have promised to offer to the temple, to divine servitude, the one to whom you shall give birth; rest assured now, my lady, that your daughter is the true temple wherein the eternal Lord and God shall be seen and worshipped. And of her shall be sung the words: "*Templum Dei sanctum est*";[4] for this temple shall be holy—of singular holiness.

'You, glorious Anne, did not ask for a daughter who was physically beautiful, for you knew that beauty was sometimes a grave danger for women; yet Our Lord God shall give her to you so beautiful that neither Eve, nor Rachel, nor Esther, nor any other woman, present or future, shall be comparable to her, for of her alone is it said that: "*Ista est speciosa inter filias Iherusalem*";[5] for she is the most beautiful of all women ever created. And this beauty shall be accompanied by such purity that on those who behold her face shall she bestow true pureness of heart and mind.

'Our Lord God commands that you give her the name Mary, which means "enlightened", for by her light shall be illuminated the entire world. She shall be the very bright star which will guide all those who sail the stormy seas of this world, and will lead them to a safe port. And this name Mary has such power *quia caelum laetatur, angeli gaudent, mundus exultat, daemones fugiunt, infernus contremiscit,*[6] because every time she is devoutly named, the entire heavens shall rejoice, angels shall feel great joy and happiness, the world shall show its immense satisfaction, devils shall take flight out of sheer terror, and Hell shall tremble from fear of her.'

On hearing that her desires would be so abundantly fulfilled, and with such praise and glory to her family, and that she was due to be the mother of such an excellent daughter, Anne's sorrow turned into sudden and singular delight; so, rejoicing with great felicity, while thanking Our Lord God for his immense mercy, she said: '*Sterilis eram, et genui exultationem et laetitiam Israel*',[7] meaning: 'O almighty Lord, may boundless thanks be

---

[4] 1 Corinthians 3:17.

[5] Responsory often sung on the Feasts of the Nativity of Mary (8th September) and the Assumption of the Blessed Virgin Mary (15th August).

[6] Raymundus Iordanus, Abbas Cellensis, *Contemplationes de B. Virgine*, Pars 4, Contemplatio 1, n. 2: 'caelum ridet, terra laetatur, angeli congaudent, daemones contremiscunt et infernus turbatur', in *Summa aurea de laudibus beatissimae virginis Mariae*, 13 vols., edited by J.-P. Migne and J.-J. Bourassé, Paris, 1866-1868, Vol. 4, col. 889.

[7] From the *Gospel of Pseudo-Matthew*, Chapter 5.

given to you, for I was barren, yet it pleased Your Majesty that I should conceive and give birth to her who is destined to be the delight and joy of all Israel.'

So the angel, bidding her farewell, said to her: 'Lady Anne, hurry to the golden gate, for your beloved husband is very nearby.' So she, departing very swiftly from her house with an indescribable longing to see him, went to the golden gate and there awaited her husband, who was already in view. And once Joachim had arrived, and Anne had curtsied to him, they embraced each other most lovingly. Her husband then taking her by the arm, they returned to their abode, each relating to the other with great fervour and devotion the visions they had had of the angel. And they continued their virtuous lives in great joy and satisfaction.

And on account of her age, when Anne realised that she was pregnant, she felt great pleasure and delight, and thus did she pass the nine months, with an insatiable desire to see that holy daughter whom she bore in her womb.

This glorious feast day of the Conception should be celebrated with great devotion by Christians, since it represents the beginning of our salvation. *Quia non est verus amator virginis Mariae qui respuit colere diem eius conceptionis*, for, without a doubt, whoever fails to show great respect towards or is not concerned to honour the day of her Holy Conception does not truly love the Virgin Mary, Our Queen and Lady, for she has shown herself by various miracles to be greatly pleased by the service rendered to her on such a day.

III

WHEN NINE MONTHS had passed, the glorious Anne gave birth to that excellent daughter of whom it had been said: '*Orietur stella ex Iacob*',[1] for that star must be revealed to the world, brighter than the sun, descending from the house of Jacob, and bringing joy to all creation.

And when they had swaddled her, they placed her in the arms of her mother, who, seeing that face so keenly desired, rejoiced with untold pleasure; and, kissing her with great delight, said: '*O filia mea, super solem et lunam pulcherrima, gratias ago Deo meo qui te video*', meaning: 'O daughter of mine, more beautiful by far than the sun or the moon! Boundless thanks do I offer to my Lord and God for having been considered worthy to see you and hold you in my arms!'

Once the news of the glorious birth was known, *vicini et cognati eius congratulabantur ei, quia magnificavit Dominus misericordiam suam cum illa:*[2] neighbours and kinsfolk were greatly delighted by it, for they knew that Our Lord God had exalted and extolled his mercy and grace in her, and shown her a singular kind of love, by giving her such an excellent daughter; about whom all those who visited her said: '*Erit tibi gaudium et exultatio et in nativitate eius multi gaudebunt*',[3] meaning: 'O Lady Anne,

[1] Num. 24:17.
[2] Luke 1:58.
[3] Luke 1:14.

many congratulations on your holy daughter, who shall be a singular
delight and joy to you; and many shall rejoice at her birth, engaging in a
singular celebration on the same day each year! For, without doubt, you
can be sure *non est ei similis nata in mundo*,[4] for her like has never been
born nor shall be in the whole of creation.'

And while Anne was experiencing great joy and satisfaction, five
handmaids appeared there together, sent by Our Lord to accompany and
serve our newly born lady, alongside the others who were already in Our
Lady's service. And, having curtsied low, they approached to kiss the hand
of Her Highness.

The first, named Kindness, said: '*O pulchra ad intuendum, amabilis ad
contemplandum, delectabilis ad amandum*',[5] meaning: 'O my Lady, how beautiful and pleasing you are to any eyes that behold you! O how lovable you
are to those who contemplate you; and, above all, how adorable you are to
those who love you! And I, my Lady, shall be with you, soothing your royal
soul by making you gracious and affable towards every creature; for I am
commanded to do so by Our Lord God, who has sent me into your service.'

The second one, named Poverty, spoke next, saying: '*Tu es Gloria
mea, tu es vita mea, tu lumen oculorum meorum, et tu baculum senectutis
meae*',[6] meaning: 'O Excellent Lady, His Majesty, Our Lord God has sent
me to you, and I come here most willingly, for until today I have never
found a person who has freely and readily welcomed me, other than yourself; because I can truly say that you are my glory, my life, the light of my
eyes and the staff of my old age, for in the future, when the world grows
cold, by your example alone shall I be sustained and loved. Therefore,
my Lady, I give you my word that I shall never part from you throughout
your entire life.'

The third handmaid, Prudence, said: '*Conserva me, domina, quoniam
speravi in te*',[7] meaning: 'O my Lady, since Our Lord's saw fit to put me in
your service, I beg you to keep me among the wishes and desires of the
people, for those who know me are few; but I am now hopeful that,
through you, I shall be valued, honoured and loved.'

---

[4] Part of an antiphon praising the Virgin Mary from the *officium passionis Domini*
established by St Francis of Assisi.

[5] St Anselm of Canterbury, *Orationes sive Meditationes*, Oratio 7, 'Oratio ad sanctam
Mariam pro impetrando eius et Christi amore', in F. S. Schmitt (ed.), S. *Anselmi Opera
omnia*, Edinburgh, Thomas Nelson and Sons, 1946, Vol. 3, p. 21, l. 89.

[6] In part, a conflation of Psalm 37:11 (Vulgate); 38:10 (RSV-CE), and Tobit 5:23.

[7] An adaptation of Psalm 15 [16]:1.

When the fourth handmaid, Patience, arrived, she kissed Our Lady's hand, saying: '*O Domina, conforta me; non avertas sacrum aspectum tuum a me*',[8] meaning: 'O my Lady, how greatly have I longed to come into such a worthy abode! You, my Lady, shall be my comfort and aid. I beg you not to withdraw your holy and gracious presence from me, for I can only be practised by the grief-stricken and the sorrowful, and my strength would fail without your assistance, for you, my Lady, shall be the rule and exemplar of those who are patient, and through the course of their troubles no one who follows you shall abandon me.'

Approaching Our Lady, the fifth handmaid, Steadfastness, kissed her hand and said to her: '*Ego in altissimis habito et thronus meus in columna nubis*',[9] meaning: 'Until today, my Lady, I have not come down to earth, but rather my home is in the lofty heavens, and my chair sits on the clouds, for there is nothing steadfast on the said earth, everything being subject to great changeableness, and no one can be certain of his neighbour. You, my Lady, shall introduce a new practice on earth, as an example to those who seek to follow you; for you shall be steadfast and constant in all the virtues, and shall persevere in them right to the end, in continuous increase.'

And the said virtues were welcomed with great warmth by Our Lady.

Saint Anne felt ceaseless satisfaction in her soul as she touched and handled her outstanding daughter, being ever unwilling to let her out of her arms. When she was suckling, she would look upon her face the whole time with a gentleness beyond description; when she put her in bed to sleep, she would remain with a candle in her hand, observing and contemplating that sweet face it pleased her so much to see.

Eighty days having passed, the glorious Anne went to the temple, bearing her beloved daughter in her arms, in order to render thanks to Our Lord God who had given her this child, and to offer the sacrifices mandated by law.[10] And the high priest, having seen Anne approach the temple, came out to welcome her with great joy, for he knew of her very great desire to have children, since she had discussed this matter with him over and again, very tearfully relating to him her anguish, and asking him as a favour to pray to God for this intention.

---

[8] The latter part of this invocation is an incipit from a section of rewritten psalms (to Mary), known as 'Septem psalmi beatae Mariae virginis', sometimes included in books of hours in the late-fifteenth century.

[9] Cf. Ecclesiasticus [Sirach] 24:7.

[10] A woman who had given birth to a child was expected to undergo an eighty-day period of seclusion.

So, coming up to her, the aforementioned priest said: 'O Anne, may boundless thanks be given to Our Lord God, who has thus chosen to satisfy you and fulfil your honest desire! I tell you now that *multum valet deprecatio iusti assidua*,[11] for in you I see certain proof of the fact that the continuous prayers of the just person are of great worth. In your anguish you had abandoned all other remedies, and you turned exclusively to him who was able to help you, namely, Our Lord God, begging him through fervent and continuous prayer to relieve your suffering; and His Majesty has heard, satisfied and fulfilled your wish so fully, that he has given you such a distinguished daughter, *quae valet ad vos multo magis quam decem filii*, for this daughter is worth more to you by far than ten sons. You shall leave a great example in this world to those in torment, namely, that their entire refuge should lie in prayer, if they wish to have full and speedy satisfaction.'

Anne, deeply pleased by the words of the said priest, in her heart continually gave thanks to Our Lord God for the mercy he had shown to her. And while discussing these issues, they went up to the altar, and there Anne made her offering with great devotion. And once the sacrifice, as mandated by law, was over, the glorious Anne, having bade farewell to the priest, returned to her house and placed her sweet little daughter in her cradle so that she might rest and sleep for a while. And she remained at her side, kneeling, and kissing her tiny feet and hands with untold joy. Yet even though she could not talk, Our Most Humble Lady, being unable to bear her mother's performance of such services, showed on her little face that she did not like such things. Becoming aware of her child's wishes, however, her virtuous mother, who thought of nothing else apart from pleasing her excellent daughter, put a stop to her own pleasure in order to satisfy her child; and thereafter she did not kiss her hands or feet, but only her little mouth, forehead and cheeks, with the greatest love and reverence, since she knew who this child was; for she loved her much more for her very many virtues, than for being her daughter.

[11] James 5:16.

IV

ALREADY AT SUCH an early age did this glorious virgin lead a life so well-ordered that she was a great source of wonder to whomever looked upon her, for on certain days of the week she suckled but once, knowing that fasting and penance constituted the life of the soul, as is written in the following words: '*Ista est salus animae, restauratio virtutum, via iustorum, refectio bonorum*', for the said penance is the salvation of the soul, the restoration and preservation of the virtues, the path of the righteous, the reinstatement and revival of all that is good. Our Lady, therefore, adopted and loved such penance from the beginning of her life, so as to set an example to her servants that they may follow in her footsteps, if they wish to attain the repose she enjoys.

The said lady busied herself with continuous prayer, for her mother often found her with her hands pressed together, her eyes turned heavenward, revealing in her bearing *quia in Domino delectabatur, et angelica fruebatur dulcedine*, for her spirit delighted entirely in the Lord, sensing and savouring God's sweetness, which is the repose and joy of the holy angels.

In the morning and in the evening Our Lady engaged in the loftiest contemplation, in keeping with the counsel of her devout ancestor David, who states: '*Ad vesperum demorabitur fletus, et ad matutinum laetitia*',[1] for in the evening she contemplated and reflected upon the pains and sufferings of human nature, and how it had fallen from its former heights of grace and come under its Creator's wrath, and how much damage and injury, both corporeal and spiritual, it had incurred for this reason. And this tormented her compassionate soul so terribly that the tears she shed were copious enough to dissolve her heart and mind, even as she pleaded for mercy from Our Lord God that he might see fit to remedy and heal that cruel ailment and affliction passed down by infection from Adam and extending to all his children. The shame of this infection had closed the Gates of Paradise, and there was no one on earth capable of opening them up thereto nor of washing away the disgrace thereof, unless Our Lady assisted in this task, for, in the absence of her power and wisdom, nothing beneficial to the salvation of men could be achieved.[2]

In such charitable prayer did Our Lady remain for most of the night, constantly shedding secret and closely concealed tears, yet in the firm belief that she would obtain what she had been requesting; and this made her turn her tears into very great joy and sweetness at divine goodness.

Thus, when dawn broke, she would send her soul to those joys of Paradise, and there would she contemplate the divine excellences and experience such lofty secrets and immense delights that she was forced to say: '*Parasti mihi cenaculum grande stratum, ut faciam apud te pascha*',[3] meaning: 'O eternal Lord and God, you have invited me into this room within your palace, adorned as it is with your divine presence which glorifies and cheers all those who look upon and contemplate you, and there, Lord, do you wish me to celebrate a great feast with you, in which you communicate to me your joys and sweetnesses, from which, my Lord, I would not wish to be parted for a single moment.' And, when she considered that this place of such sovereign bliss was shut and closed on account of Adam's sin, she broke into floods of endless tears, begging God's mercy to put an end to this exile of Adam and of his children, and to bring them back to his grace and love.

---

[1] Psalm 29 [30]:6.

[2] In connection with this passage, one should remember that the word for 'salvation' (Cat. *salut*) in some Romance languages also carries the (now perhaps more primary) sense of physical and/or spiritual 'health'.

[3] Thomas à Kempis, *De imitatione Christi*, 4.12.

And in this entreaty did Our Lady persist, until she might deserve to obtain what she had been requesting. We can say, therefore, that Our Lord God caused her to be born in this world so that she might be an advocate for human nature and a sanctuary for all its needs, to whom all those in torment may say with great confidence: '*Potens est misericordia tua, gratiam desideratam mihi praestare*',[4] meaning: 'O Lady, so great is the power of your mercy, that you are able to give to me the grace I desire, since from your mercy nobody who has faith departs empty-handed.'

And the more Our Lady grew, all the more did the joy of her most holy mother Anne increase, who took endless delight in beholding her and contemplating her. And when her daughter began to walk, Anne would take her by her tiny hands and help her, with such love and reverence that it seemed to her that in touching and beholding her child, she received additional grace each time. But Anne felt such pleasure in serving her that to take a rest made her feel sad, and, therefore, she was always considering what she might do for her.

And when Our Lady began to talk, Anne was filled with singular joy, so wishing to share this with her husband Joachim, she called out to him with great happiness, saying: '*Venite, audite, et vivet anima vestra*',[5] meaning: 'Come, Lord Joachim, and you shall hear the clever words of your beloved daughter, and your soul shall flourish by way of the incalculable satisfaction you shall draw from hearing her speak.'

So Joachim, arriving with singular joy, and hearing Our Lady, his daughter, call him 'father' in that angelic voice, almost lost his mind with inestimable delight and ran to embrace her. Raising her on high, he said: '*Quis ad fontem suavitatis accedens, non modicum suavitatis inde reportat?*'[6], meaning: 'O my lady and daughter, who can possibly approach you, who are a fount of sweetness and gentleness, and not be left with a unique sense of pleasure in his soul, just as I now feel in hearing you and seeing you and holding you in my arms? You are the delight of my family, the repose of my old age! I shall now depart this mortal life in peace, since I shall acquire such a glorious reputation for having been the father of such an outstanding daughter.'

And when her father left her, her mother would take her, and thus did they both rejoice in that blessed daughter.

---

[4] *Ibid.*, 4.14.

[5] Isaiah 55:3.

[6] Thomas à Kempis, *De imitatione Christi*, 4.04.

O worthy beyond doubt of great veneration are the father and mother who have brought such a jewel into this world! And we may say the following, in praise and exaltation of Our Lady: '*Benedicti sint pater et mater qui te genuerunt, quorum memoria permanebit in aeternum*',[7] meaning: 'O Lady, how deeply is the world obliged to laud and praise your father and mother who have begotten you, the memory of whom shall remain immortal throughout all present and future generations!'

[7] Part of the Office of the Immaculate Virgin Mary, attributed to St Bonaventure.

LXI

STILL VERY HAPPY after all the celebrations, Our Lady recalled what the angel had said about her dear first cousin, who was six months pregnant, so she decided to go to visit her. She communicated her decision to her beloved handmaids, one of whom, named Diligence, replied: '*Bonum opus nunquam differendum est*', meaning: 'O my Lady, you already know that good deeds and holy thoughts should not be postponed, but rather should immediately be put into effect, so, therefore, I beg you to carry out your decision without delay.'

The most beloved of her handmaids, named Holy Charity, then rose to her feet, saying to her: 'My lady, I shall go with you in order to serve Elizabeth in her childbirth and in all her other needs, for I am sure that you will stay in her company throughout the three months which remain until she gives birth.'

So Our Lady, wishing to proceed with her journey, emerged from the bedroom in which she had been enclosed and moved into the room where Joseph was, in order to ask his permission to leave, for, since Our Lord had given him to her as a husband, she wished to be obedient to him in all things. But when Joseph had listened to her, he told her that he was very happy for her to go, and that he wished to accompany her. And so, Our Lady left her house, with Humility and Poverty leading her by the arm, while Holy Modesty went first to show her the byroads, so that people would not see her ladyship; and thus did she reach the house of Zechariah without having met anyone on the way.

The said Zechariah was taking a stroll at that time near the entrance to his house and, seeing Our Lady enter his residence so unexpectedly, was greatly astonished and felt singular joy. So, after he had bowed to her, he hurried to the bedroom to convey the good news to his wife by means of signs, since he was unable to speak. His wife then quickly emerged from the room, and seeing Our Lady, her first cousin, whom she loved so dearly, was filled with such great happiness and satisfaction that she was unable to move from where she stood.

And Our Most Humble Lady and Mother of God quickened her step in order to approach Elizabeth and, with great delight on her face, greeted her in the following words: '*Gaudium tibi sit semper, cognata dilectissima*',[1] meaning: 'O most beloved cousin, may you always be joyful, for you have been worthy to conceive a son such as the one with whom you have been pregnant for six months! For, of this be sure, the Son of God is coming to visit him, with the aim of sanctifying him in your womb and of cleansing him of original sin, for of him may it be said in particular: "*Ante sanctus quam natus; prius plenus Deo quam natus ex matre; prius noscens Deum quam notus in mundo*",[2] meaning that this your glorious son shall be of such distinction that he shall be a saint even before he emerges from your womb, and he shall be filled with the grace and love of Our Lord prior to being born from you, his mother, and he shall know and love God to a singular degree prior to being born into this world and known thereby.'

Et factum est, ut audivit salutationem Mariae Elizabeth, exultavit infans in utero eius,[3] for as soon as Elizabeth heard the melody and sweetness of that soft voice belonging to the Blessed Virgin Mary, her infant rejoiced with untold delight within the womb of the said mother, knowing that all his lady aunt had said applied to him, and so, enclosed within the womb, and seeing before him His Divine Majesty clad in human flesh, he knelt to

---

[1] Cf. Tobit 5:11.

[2] Possibly a conflation of a responsorium from St Bernard of Clairvaux, *Sermones de Sanctis. Officium de Sancto Victore Confessore* (PL 183: 776D), and St Anselm of Canterbury, *Orationes sive Meditationes*, Oratio 8, 'Oratio ad sanctum Iohannem Baptistam', ed. cit., Vol. 3, p. 26, ll. 4-5.

[3] Luke 1:41.

worship him, giving thanks with boundless happiness and joy for the ever so singular graces bestowed upon him.

Elizabeth felt the great joy and satisfaction that her infant was experiencing within her womb, *repleta est Spiritu Sancto Elizabeth*,[4] for the said Elizabeth was filled with that peculiar delight deriving from the Holy Spirit which cannot be spoken or put into words, and which is something that the human heart cannot stand for long, because Elizabeth felt compelled to let out a loud cry mingled with a great flood of tears brought on by her extraordinary happiness, when she said: '*Benedictus tu in mulieribus et benedictus fructus ventris tui.*'[5] By this she meant: 'O, blessed are you, my Lady, of singular blessedness, among all women created or still to be so, and blessed be the unrivalled fruit of your glorious womb, which has come into the world in order to sate the hunger of human nature!

'*Et unde hoc mihi ut veniat mater Domini mei ad me?*[6] Whence comes to me, then, my Lady, such grace and mercy, that you, who are the mother of my Lord and Redeemer, should visit me, unworthy as I am of such a unique advantage? O my Lady, blessed are you and worthy of all praise, for you have firmly believed the divine mystery proclaimed to you by the angel, and therefore, my Lady, in you shall be fulfilled and accomplished all of the things said to you in the name of Our Lord God.'

And Our Most Humble Lady, seeing her cousin thus filled with the Holy Spirit say such lofty things to her praise and glory, and wishing to return and refer all that praise and exaltation to His Divine Majesty, knelt down with her eyes turned heavenward and her hands pressed together, and said with the greatest devotion: '*Magnificat anima mea Dominum. Et exultavit spiritus meus in Deo salutari meo*'.[7] By this she meant: 'You, my cousin, extol me in thoughts and in words, while within your womb your infant moves with manifestations of untold joy, celebrating my arrival, yet my soul magnifies, exalts, praises and glorifies my Lord and Creator, and my spirit rejoices and delights in God alone, who is my Saviour and my Life.'

Once she had finished her most devout canticle, Our Lady rose to her feet, and her cousin Elizabeth then took her very reverently by the hand and led her to a concealed room, begging her to rest there from the labours of her journey. Zechariah then took hold of the glorious Joseph

---

[4] *Idem.*
[5] Lines from the *Ave Maria.*
[6] Luke 1:43.
[7] Luke 1:46-47; also the opening lines of the *Magnificat* or 'Canticle of Mary'.

and, with great joy, led him with him; but even though Zechariah was mute, he showed the satisfaction he felt within his soul at the presence of Our Lord, of Our Lord's mother and of that distinguished old man who, among all mortals, was deemed worthy of being chosen to be the spouse and guardian of Our Most Serene Lady Queen, mother of the Eternal King. And so, in great love and charity, these holy people stayed in the house of Zechariah until the time arrived when Elizabeth gave birth.

On how Joseph, realising that Our Lady was pregnant, decided to leave her secretly, and on how he
received assurances from the angel regarding the
mystery of the Incarnation of the Son of God

LXIII

As Our Lord grew within his mother's womb, Joseph began to realise
that Our Lady was pregnant, and he became very upset since he did not
know what had caused the said pregnancy, despite the fact that he was so
convinced of the purity and saintliness of Our Lady, *quia possibilius enim
credebat virginem sine viro posse concipere, quam Mariam posse peccare,*[1] for it
seemed more feasible to him that a virgin might conceive in the absence
of a man than that the Lady Mary could sin or be at fault in any respect.

So, on account of the great love and reverence he felt towards her, he
never dared to ask her what kind of pregnancy hers was; instead, he
became flustered and struggled continually with his thoughts, while con-
cealing his sadness as best he could. His troubled expression, however,
could not escape the attention of Our Lady, who knew full well how perturbed he felt in his mind at not knowing the manner of her pregnancy,
whereby she felt great anguish and compassion for the saintly old man,

---

[1] Ludolph of Saxony, *Vita Jesu Christi*, Part I, Chapter 8, citing Chrysostom. Cf. *Eru-
diti commentarii in Evangelium Mattheae incerto auctore*, Homily 1, *Opus imperfectus* (PG
56: 633).

whom she loved dearly, seeing him distressed by something at which he would rejoice so fully if only he were to know about it. So she turned to God's mercy, by way of devout and fervent prayer, begging His Majesty to reveal to this holy man his divine mystery, namely, that of his Son made man, for she dared not divulge this secret to anyone without the express permission of His Royal Excellency, for she knew that it was written that: '*Sacramentum regis abscondere bonum est.*'[2]

And since Our Lady continued her prayers, she was deemed worthy of obtaining what she had requested, for Joseph, whose sorrows carried on growing and increasing, had decided to leave her and secretly to go away, as he was unable to provide people with any explanation for her pregnancy. So, on entering his room in order to take his cloak, while thinking that forever would he have to be parted from such a dear and kindly companion, he felt such acute anguish that, emitting the loudest of wails, he fell to the ground, and there remained for most of the night, crying throughout. At dawn, exhausted by his great sorrow, he briefly fell asleep. *Ecce angelus Domini in somnis apparuit ei, dicens: 'Ioseph, fili David, noli timere.*'[3] But the angel sent by Our Lord God appeared to him in a dream, saying: 'Joseph, son of David, have no fear, for you, who descend from the most faithful House of David, are in no doubt about the great promises made to your ancestors concerning how the true Messiah is to be made incarnate in a virgin and to be born from her as God and man without loss of her virginity, and therefore your ancestor David, contemplating the exaltation of his stock, said with sovereign joy: "*Dixit Dominus Domino meo: Sede a dextris meis*",[4] meaning that Our Lord God and Father, who is universal lord over all, had told his Son that he may sit at his right hand. This Son, insofar as he is God, is equal to his Father who is Lord of David and of all other men, and, insofar as he is man, shall be a son of David, and therefore calls him "my Lord", for to David has this been promised and granted.

'And, if a virgin is to be mother of this Lord, rest assured that it is your wife, true daughter of David. *Ubi vidisti tam dignam? Ubi vidisti tam pulchram? Ubi vidisti tam sanctam?*[5] Tell me, Joseph, have you seen any woman, among those past, present or future, as worthy as she of being the Mother of God? And have you seen her like in corporeal or spiritual beauty, and do you

---

[2] Tobit 12:17.

[3] Matthew 1:20.

[4] Psalm 109 [110]:1.

[5] Cf. St Anselm of Canterbury (incertus), *Sermo de conceptione beatae Mariae* (PL 159: 320C).

know of anyone who equals her in saintliness? What is it you doubt? Put all sadness to one side. *Accipe Mariam coniugem tuam: quod enim in ea natum est, de Spiritu Sancto est.*[6] Joseph, accept this lady, Mary, not only as your wife, but also as your Queen and Lady, for she is the mother of the eternal God, and her pregnancy owes thanks to the Holy Spirit. *Pariet autem filium, et vocabis nomen eius Iesum.*[7] She shall give birth to an excellent son, to whom you, as father, must assign a name and whom you must call Jesus, for you have obtained this singular honour from Our Lord God, namely, that you on earth may be called the father of his Son. *Ipse enim salvum faciet populum suum a peccatis eorum.*[8] Do not doubt then that this is the true redeemer of human nature, who, with his own blood, shall save his people, by offering bounteous satisfaction for its sins through his death.'

Joseph, thus informed by the angel, raised himself up with boundless joy and knelt on the ground to thank His Divine Majesty for the mercy shown to him, saying: '*Gratias tibi ago, Domine, quia convertisti planctum meum in gaudium mihi*',[9] meaning: 'I give you thanks, my Lord God, for the way in which, by your infinite mercy and goodness, you have so generously turned my sorrow and tears into happiness and joy.'

Leaving his room in great haste, he went to the small cell where Our Lady was, and he found her kneeling, surrounded by such brightness and light that he could not make her out on account of the very great radiance of her face. So, falling to the ground, with a loud cry and many tears, he said: 'O Excellent Lady, forgive me, for I, who am unworthy of your company, had decided to leave you, unaware that you were the Mother of the Son of God! Now, my Lady, having been informed of your rank, I beg you to pardon and forgive me for this error and to accept me as your servant, for hereafter, my Lady, shall my entire life be taken up by serving his lordship your son and your ladyship.'

Our Merciful Lady, feeling great compassion for the saintly old man, went swiftly to him and, her eyes brimming with tears, raised him up from the floor, saying that she forgave him only too gladly and that she had suffered great anguish at his distress, and that he should be cheerful, since Our Lord had reassured him so fully by revealing to him the secret mystery of the Incarnation. And she made Joseph sit down on a bench so that he might rest a little from the past days of sorrow, and in order to make him

---

[6] Matthew 1:20.
[7] Matthew 1:21.
[8] *Idem.*
[9] Cf. Psalm 29:12 [30:11].

happy, she started to tell him in sequence the entire mystery of her pregnancy and the great mysteries which thereafter were to follow. Joseph listened to this with such devotion and disturbance of thought that he almost lost his mind, shedding continuous tears.

And they frequently had conversations of this kind during the nine months, for they never talked of anything else apart from how they would welcome Our Lord, how they would treat him, and with how much love and reverence they would serve him; and in speaking and thinking about this lay their mutual delight. And thus did they spend that entire period awaiting the appearance of the Son of God so fervently desired.

On how Our Lord emerged from the virginal
womb of his mother and was worshipped and
swaddled by her

LXV

THE NIGHT of the Sunday on which the Son of God was to be introduced
to the world having arrived, Our Lady knelt down, raising her thoughts to
the divine heights, and contemplating the wondrous mysteries of human
redemption, whereupon untold secrets were communicated to her soul.
So, inflamed with supreme love for her son, and wishing to see him with
her bodily eyes, she spoke to him in her mind with supreme gentleness,
saying: '*O pulcherrimum et dulcissimum Dominum meum! Ex toto corde meo te
desidero! Veni mihi! Videam te, speciosissime prae filiis hominum, quia amore
langueo et te videre desidero!*',[1] meaning: 'O my Lord and most beloved,
beautiful and sweet son, you know that I sincerely desire you! Come to me!
Let me see you and hold you in my lap, most beautiful above all the sons
of men, for my soul already languishes from its insatiable desire to see your
presence!'

And as midnight approached, while Our Lady remained thus, wholly
absorbed in and inflamed with divine love and the desire to see her most

---

[1] The phrase 'speciosissime prae filiis hominum' derives from Psalm 44 [45]:3, while
that of 'quia amore langueo' occurs in the Song of Solomon 5:8.

beloved son, the great prince Saint Michael appeared along with all the heavenly court, and kneeling down in front of her ladyship, they kissed her hand, all in sequence, as Queen and Lady of the Kingdom of Heaven, and that place shone with a singular radiance. The said prince, Saint Michael, ordered the entire throng to stand around Our Excellent Lady—who was soon to give birth—playing various musical instruments of singular harmoniousness, while her ladyship knelt in their midst, her hands pressed together, her eyes turned heavenward, and her face resplendent and thoroughly angelic.

When Saint Michael approached, he knelt down before Her Highness, summoning his chief confidant, named Gabriel, and Prince Raphael, so that the three of them might give pleasure to Our Lady through song. Before they started, they asked Saint Joseph to do them the honour of singing the tenor part, so he rose to his feet very swiftly and approached them with great joy, saying that he was very happy to assist them in singing, for such was the delight he felt in his soul that he would gladly break the bonds of his body so that his spirit might sing and dance uninterruptedly in celebration of Our Lady and her pregnancy. And so the four of them began their song with solemnity, using the words:

> *Mariae virginis fecundat viscera*
> *vis Sacri Flaminis, non carnis opera;*
> *carens originis labe puerpera,*
> *Dei et hominis dans nova foedera.* [2]

And at this melody, the hour and time ordained by the eternal Father having approached, Our Lord emerged from the virginal womb of his mother without causing her any pain, leaving her chaste and a virgin, as David had prophesied with the words: '*Tanquam sponsus procedens de thalamo*',[3] for the said glorious David had seen in his mind how the Son of God would emerge from that excellent marriage bed constituted by his mother's purest of wombs, clad in that new garment of human nature, as that nature's spouse.

Saint Michael and the other princes swiftly took hold of Our Lord so that he should not fall to the ground, worshipping His Majesty with pro-

---

[2] A hymn to the Virgin Mary.

[3] Psalm 18:6 [19:5]; this verse was traditionally interpreted as foreshadowing the Incarnation.

found reverence and presenting him to his lady mother, who beheld him with boundless joy, and worshipped him before she had touched him, acknowledging him to be her Lord and God, attending first of all to her reverence for God rather than to her love as a mother, even though her love for him was unbounded. So, taking him from the hands of the angels, she placed him with supreme caution and reverence upon her lap, warmly embracing and kissing him with loving tenderness, as her true and natural son,[4] while Our Lord fixed his kind eyes on the face of his Most Holy Mother, seeming to take pleasure therein as something dearer to him than anything else in the world. And, though lacking the medium of language, the souls of the son and of the mother spoke to each other in such lofty and secret conversations that even the intellect of an angel would not have sufficed to comprehend them, whereby Our Lady was filled with such joy that it defied appraisal or description.

While beholding and contemplating that little body, and seeing its outstanding beauty, she knew it to be that of which David had said: '*Speciosus forma prae filiis hominum*',[5] for it was the most beautiful of all the sons of men. And as she looked upon that divine person so tender and so delicate, and remembering that he was passible and mortal, Our Lady felt within her such excessive sorrow that it passed through her entire heart, and especially when she heard him cry as a result of the cold. Accompanying him in his tears with sovereign compassion, she wrapped him up with the utmost diligence, assisted by her handmaids, for Diligence provided her with swaddling-clothes, Charity warmed them up, Poverty stretched them as far as she could in order that they might manage to cover the tiny feet of Our Lord, while Compassion[6] had brought a piece of cloth that was placed over his head.

And when Our Lady had him nicely swaddled like this, Our Lord ceased crying, indicating that he had derived pleasure from that humble outfit which spared him from the cold, and Our Lady, herself deriving great pleasure from his restful state, said to him with loving gentleness: '*Tu*

---

[4] Her true and natural son' (Cat. *fill seu verdader e natural*). Although a 'natural son' was one born of unmarried parents who were, nonetheless, at liberty to marry at the time of the child's conception or birth, it seems here that Isabel de Villena is using the term 'natural' in its ordinary sense (and in contradistinction to 'adoptive'), and more probably still, in order to emphasise the full humanity of Christ and her maternal attachment to her son. See the following paragraphs.

[5] Psalm 44 [45]:3.

[6] Cat. *pietat*.

qui terram palmo concludis involutus panniculis recreatus es',[7] meaning: 'O wondrous Son of God, you, who on account of your great power and magnificence hold the entire earth in your hand: now, my Life, are you warmed and revived by these scanty little pieces of cloth.'

Our Lady then took the tiny feet of her son, and warmed them with her own hands, lacking any other source of heat, while saying to him: 'O my darling, the great charity and love that you bear towards human nature makes you feel the cold and the scantiness of your clothing so bitterly! O my Lord, may men know this and appreciate it, and may they love you gladly, since you have loved them so dearly!'

[7] St Anselm of Canterbury, *Liber meditationum et orationum*, IX (PL 158: 750B), wherein *reclinatus* instead of *recreatus*; the passage refers to Luke 2:7.

LXXXVIII

ON ARRIVING at a city named Hermopolis, in which Our Lady decided to stay, and while passing through its suburbs, she and Joseph looked around and about for a place where they might take lodgings. And when they had searched at length, they saw a lowly dwelling close to the river, despised and detested by all the inhabitants of the said city as being unhealthy. But Our Lady thought it would be a great piece of fortune if they could rent it, so she asked to whom the house belonged, and, finding its owner, she and Joseph humbly begged him to rent it to them. This man, however, although he looked askance at them, seeing that they were foreign and poor and wearing the clothing of Jews, who were a people much abhorred by the inhabitants of that place, let them have the dwelling, being entirely convinced that no one else would take it, since it was uninhabitable; so with great fury he told them to pay the rent in its entirety first of all, otherwise they would not set foot in the house. So Our Lady replied that she would make efforts to sell the she-ass she had brought with her, and that she would pay the rent, which is precisely what she did.

From what was left over, then, from the money she had earned from the she-ass, she bought a small amount of straw from which, in a corner of the house, she fashioned a sort of bed for the honourable Joseph, and she placed the remnants elsewhere, and there would she sleep holding Our Lord, her son, in her arms, for she had no other bed on which to lay him down. Yet His Majesty slept with great pleasure in the lap of his mother, for there did not exist a bed more pleasing to him in the entire world.

O how great was the poverty and want undergone by Our Lady in that land of Egypt, particularly during the early days, for she was not known nor was anybody willing to entrust any work to her, still less to Joseph, nor were they able to earn a single penny, as a result of which they had to endure extreme hunger! For Our Lord wished them to feel all kinds of hardship in order to increase their patience, and divine power had ordained that Our Excellent Lady, and mother of his Son, should frequently suffer all kinds of discomfort and experience limitless anguish so that she might be an example to all mortals and might show great mercy towards all those who made appeals to her, for nobody is truly able to pity, to know or, still less, to describe a person's travails other than someone who has been through them. For this reason, therefore, Ecclesiasticus quite rightly says: '*Qui navigat in mari enarrat pericula eius*',[1] for whoever sails the seas knows only too well how to describe their dangers, and whoever has been greatly persecuted and suffered torment, knows only too well how to counsel and assist the tormented.

Who can conceive of the amount of sorrow by which the mind of this kind lady was afflicted when she saw Joseph, a man of venerable age, get by on such meagre provisions that he could scarcely sustain himself? But Our Lady herself very often went through the day on bread alone, so as to leave for the said Joseph the tiny portion of food they possessed.

The need and want of Our Lady extended to all things, however, for her dwelling was so lacking in all the essentials that, at night, they had no clothing with which to cover themselves apart from that alone in which they were clad. As a result, during the night Our Lady very frequently heard the virtuous old man let out great moans on account of the harsh pains he was suffering as a result of the cold, whilst she, pierced through with the utmost compassion, would offer him the blanket that was covering her up. Yet this glorious and eminent man, trembling from the severe cold, would reply: 'O my Lady, don't do that, for I should like to shed all the clothes I am wearing in order to give them to you, for I suffer greater distress by far because of the cold I know you to feel than because of my own.'

---

[1] Ecclesiasticus [Sirach] 43:24 (43:26).

But, however pronounced they were, all of Our Lady's afflictions could be endured apart from that innermost pity which plagued her heart when contemplating God's Son and hers in a state of such poverty that he was in great need of all the essential things!

Nor, as he grew, did Our Lady have new clothes into which she might change him; God's mercy, rather, granted that a child's purple gown she had made for him grew just as he did, and served him in infancy and adulthood as well as throughout his entire life. Nor did she have enough money to buy him any little shoes, but rather, when Our Lord began to walk, Our Lady would not dare put him on the ground, as his feet were bare; instead, she first spread her cloak on the floor, and helped Our Lord to walk around on it, holding him by his tiny hands, although not allowing him to walk further than the cloak stretched, so that his tiny feet should not get cold.

O who shall not love poverty, given that Our Eternal King has suffered so much in a variety of ways which would defy description?

LXXXIX

AMID THE HARDSHIPS and exertions that Our Lady endured during her stay in Egypt she experienced the most intense joy, and that was when her beloved son began to talk. The first word he uttered was to call Our Lady 'mother' with such loving gentleness that her soul was so filled with the utmost satisfaction that she said: '*Anima mea liquefacta est, ut dilectus locutus est mihi!*',[1] meaning: 'My soul melts away from the greatest of joy, for my beloved has spoken to me.'

And Her Highness embraced that divine son, kissing him over and over again with supreme satisfaction, and saying to him: '*O aeterna veritas et vera caritas! Quam dulcia faucibus meis eloquia tua!*',[2] meaning: 'O eternal truth, and true and perfect charity, how sweet are your words to me!'

And every time Our Lord called her 'mother', new joy was kindled in the heart of Our Lady so that she was obliged to say: '*Gloria mea semper innovabitur*',[3] meaning: 'O, my Life, how my glory and joy always grow and

---

[1] Song of Solomon 5:6.
[2] The first part of this quotation comes from St Augustine, *Confessiones*, Book VII, Chapter 10.16; the second, from Psalm 118 [119]:103.
[3] Job 29:20.

increase when I am called "mother" by you.' For this is the great excellence and singular glory of our Queen and Lady, in other words, that she be called the Mother of God and so named by His Majesty. On account of this sole honour does she warrant all the rest, insofar as Her Highness's servants who find themselves in a position of need, and who turn to her in the hope of obtaining what they request, say to her with great confidence:

Monstra te esse matrem,
sumat per te preces
qui pro nobis natus
tulit esse tuus.[4]

And so agreeable to Our Lord, her son, is this prayer that, showing himself to obey Our Lady as his dearest mother, he will liberally grant all things to those who with true faith and devotion offer it to her, for her glory and honour belongs to her son, and those who call upon his mother are heard and succoured very swiftly by her son.

[4] Lines from the *Ave Maris Stella*, a plainsong Vespers hymn to Mary, dating from at least the eighth century.

XC

SO OUR LADY, wishing to communicate to Joseph the great joy she had
felt when Our Lord, her son, began to talk, called out: *'Venite et audite quia
Dominus locutus est'*, meaning: 'Come, Joseph, and you shall be delighted,
for you shall hear Our Lord, my son, who can already speak.' So he, arriving with inestimable joy, approached Our Lady and took the King of
Heaven from her arms, and with the most loving fervour raised him on
high, while starting to dance him about, and said to him: *'Loquere, Domine,
et audiat servus tuus! Sonet vox tua in auribus meis!'*,[1] meaning: 'Speak, my
Lord, and let your servant hear you; let the sweetness of your voice sound
in my ears, and I shall derive repose from all my hardships.' So Our Lord,
looking into his face with a playful smile, and placing his tiny hands on
Joseph's head, said to him, falteringly: 'Father'.

O who can gauge how great was the sweetness felt by Joseph's soul
when he heard such a word! Or how much rest and repose he derived from

---

[1] Song of Solomon 2:14.

all his hardships! And out of intense joy he shed profuse tears, while saying: 'O infinite goodness! How pleasing it is, that I should hear from Your Majesty such a charming word! All the anguish and hardships that I might undergo are a joy to me, since I have been, my Lord, so beloved and favoured by you. O my Lord, how much more uplifting and cheering is the solace you offer than all the delights, pleasures and successes that can be experienced in this world! O my Life, how wealthy and well-provided I am, holding you in my arms! All the pleasures and successes of this wretched life would be abhorred by mortals if the latter were to feel even a hint of solace from you!'

And Our Excellent Lady, watching the joy and satisfaction expressed by Joseph, felt great comfort and contentment, so she said to him: 'O Joseph, it is pleasing to love and serve this Lord who liberally and abundantly pays and rewards his servants, by giving them *pro terrenis caelestia, pro temporalibus sempiterna, pro modicis magna,*[2] since in return for worldly things forsaken out of love for him, he gives celestial; for temporal things, eternal; and for the least hardship, infinite repose.'

And so, Our Lady and Joseph, deriving such solace from the Son of God, underwent the poverty and hardship of their foreign travels, and the more Our Lord grew, the more clearly did he speak, for in all things human he wished to be similar to other men, and Our Lady became even happier, hearing the divine words of her beloved son.

---

[2] St Cyprian of Carthage (†258), *Liber de opere et eleemosynis*, XXVI (PL 4: 621A).

XCI

OUR LADY did not wean her son until he was three years old, because she did not have the delicacies which other mothers are in the habit of giving their children when they wean them prematurely; instead, such was the want and need of Our Lady that, when Our Lord was young, he would sometimes ask for food and yet she would have nothing in her entire house to give him apart from a small piece of bread. O what a knife of sorrow[1] that was to her, and with what tears she would reply to him, saying: 'My Life, I have nothing to give you.' So thereafter, every day at dinner time, Our Lady would set aside a small amount of bread so that she might be able to give her beloved son some breakfast and lunch, as the tenderness of his age demanded.

---

[1] I have chosen to retain this striking and immediate figure of speech (which is echoed a few lines below) rather than to replace it with something along the lines of 'source of anguish', since the same image also recurs, in Chapter CCXLII, in a slightly extended form, in a passage describing Mary Magdalene's grief at finding the tomb of Christ to be empty.

XCII

When Our Lady began to be known by the women of that land, they gave her work as a spinster and seamstress, and by means of the said jobs she earned some money, from which she lived, and with the remainder she bought certain small utensils for use in her house. Joseph, likewise, worked as a carpenter and blacksmith, hiring himself out to the masters of that art until he had obtained a reasonable sum of money.

O who can conceive of the degree of sorrow by which Our Kind Lady's heart was pierced through when she saw that venerable old man go to work for unfamiliar households, in which he suffered severe reproaches and insults, and yet when he returned home in the evening, aching and tired, she would have nothing to give him for dinner! In great anguish and distress, therefore, Our Lady often shed endless tears out of compassion for the great need and want which the saintly old man was undergoing, whereas he moaned and complained much more about her suffering than about his own want. Accordingly, the said Joseph, in order to raise Our Lady's spirits and to give her company within the house, decided to stop putting himself up for hire, so he bought a small amount of old tim-

ber with the money he had earned from his various days' labour and thereafter he worked from home, selling his wares from the doorway.

And, as Our Lord grew, he began to work and to assist Joseph as much
as he could, given his age, and he served his lady mother in every respect
that other children were accustomed to serving their mothers. And when
Our Lady would not let him serve her out of consideration for the fact that
he was the Son of God and her Creator, His Majesty would say to her: 'O
my lady mother, allow me to do it, for I wish to set an example to men, who
are dust and ashes, so that they may learn to humble themselves and not
feel shame at performing deeds of service out of love for me, while bearing in mind that I have abhorred all those things which in themselves bring
honour and esteem, and that I have applied myself to those which
wretched pride avoids and detests. For you, my lady mother, know that
I have said to you on various occasions: "*Non veni ministrari sed ministrare*",[1]
since I did not come into the present world to be served, but rather
to serve.'

So Our Lady, who realised that this was the desire of her beloved son,
with great pity and sorrow allowed him to do what he wanted, especially in
the presence of strangers, so that they should not say that he was badly
brought up. And Our Lord went out of the house for all the essential
things, for his lady mother had no one else to serve her.

He brought her water from the spring, and he went with the other
young boys to gather firewood, carrying it on his shoulders. And Our Kind
Lady, who saw him arriving thus tired and sweating, would come out to
meet him with arms outstretched, and swiftly relieving him of his burden
and placing him on her lap, while kissing him with great warmth, she
would very lovingly wipe the little beads of sweat from his brow, and,
bathing his divine face in tears, would say: 'O my Life, do you wish to
exhaust yourself like this at such a young age? O my Lord and son, how *your*
efforts tire *me* out! Rest, my love, if you wish me to be at my ease.' And Our
Lord, in order to give peace and satisfaction to his lady mother, would converse with her for a while, and when he had had a rest, started working
again with Joseph, wishing never to be idle, and demonstrating how he
enjoyed being virtuously and continuously occupied.

And when his lady mother had finished a pound of worsted or of flax,
Our Lord would return it to those from whom it came. Yet those coarse
and ill-natured people of Egypt would give him such a frosty reception that

[1] Matthew 20:28; Mark 10:45.

they often threw him out of their house, not wishing to pay him the price of the work he had brought. So Our Lord, very patiently keeping his peace, would return to the home where his mother was, while Our Lady, on seeing him, could tell from his expression that he had been given a poor welcome at whichever place he had gone, despite his not mentioning anything, and would take him by the hand, and bringing him indoors, would say to him with tears aplenty: 'O repose of the afflicted, who has dared to upset you? O joy of angels, who has brought sadness to your divine face? From now on, my son, you shall not go to return the work, but I shall go instead, for I should prefer them to abuse and to eject me than you, my Life, since the insults you receive are much harder for me to bear than those I receive myself.'

So Our Merciful Lord replied to his beloved mother, saying: 'O mother of mine, worry not, for it is with a view to suffering insults and contempt that I have come into this world of mortals, and I choose to encourage my servants to suffer their insults gladly, by saying to them: "*Libenter suffertis insipientes, cum sitis ipsi sapientes. Sustinetis enim si quis vos in servitutem redigit, si quis devorat, si quis accipit, si quis extollitur, si quis in faciem vos caedit*",[2] giving them to understand: "Those who wish to follow me, do not doubt that of necessity you must gladly bear the insults which will be thrown at you by those lacking in wisdom, and thus shall you demonstrate your own wisdom and good sense; tolerate likewise the fact that they make use of you as they would people who are subject to them, even when they reveal that they wish to obliterate and destroy you. Let nothing frighten you, and if they strike you in the face, accept it with pleasure and delight, for this is the sure and certain path by which to get to Paradise."

'And if, my lady mother, I fail to put these things into practice, but instead preach them alone, my preaching would be little valued, and therefore I wish it to be said of me: "*Coepit Iesus facere et docere*",[3] for I shall first put into practice what I wish to reveal in words. Thus, my mother, resign yourself to the fact that my entire life shall be accompanied by a wide range of torments, and that it is in terms of such suffering that you are to have possession of me in the present life.'

On hearing these arguments from the lips of her beloved son, Our Lady, without further reply, shed boundless tears, leaving all things to his ordinance and will.

---

[2] 2 Corinthians 11:19.
[3] Acts 1:1.

Part Two: Women during the Apostolic
Life of Christ

ON HOW OUR LORD, WHILE PREACHING IN JERUSALEM,
CONVERTED THE GREAT AND NOBLE LADY MAGDALENE
BY DRAWING HER TOWARDS THE LOVE AND KNOWLEDGE
OF HIMSELF

CXVII

WHILE OUR LORD was preaching in Jerusalem, it came to pass that a grand and very wealthy lady, more singular in beauty and grace than all the ladies of her estate, as well as free from the governance of her father and mother—since they had already died, leaving great riches and an abundance of goods to her, for despite the fact that she had a brother and a sister, she was the principal lady and the eldest of all—, thus became a free citizen during her youth, without anyone to reproach her. So, taking her own desire as law, she followed all her sensual appetites, focusing exclusively on the pleasures and enjoyment of her body, and on dresses and new fashions. Furthermore, nothing was difficult for her, since she had money to spend, for an abundance of wealth in a young person is a great opportunity for sinfulness, as Solomon testifies when he says: '*Si dives fueris, non eris immunis a delicto*',[1] meaning that a wealthy person does not stand exempt from a great number of trespasses.

[1] Ecclesiasticus [Sirach] 11:10.

And this lady loved to hold festivities and to devise outfits. She had a large hall and a salon in her house where all the young ladies intent on pleasure and enjoyment would congregate, and wherein parties and banquets would be held every day. And since in such matters the reputation of ladies cannot remain intact, even if their deeds be not unworthy, such displays raise suspicions of evildoing and licence among maligners, leading the latter to judge and condemn the lives of such people, who think more about satisfying their disordered desires than of preserving their reputations. So, the nobler the estate of this lady and the more singular her beauty and wealth, the sooner was her reputation sullied. And the lower classes, who generally delight in speaking ill of great ladies for the slightest reason they can find, talked at such great length about this lady, whose name was Mary Magdalene, that before long the townsfolk simply called her 'the sinner woman'.

And while this noble Magdalene remained caught up in her zeal for these gatherings of hers, the great repute of Our Lord's preaching began to spread. And when one day in her presence there was talk of the beautiful eloquence of Our Lord and of how the divine words of His Majesty would suddenly change the wishes and intentions of men from ill to good, as well as of how he performed deeds so wondrous that everybody was astounded, the said Magdalene, having heard this, was so inflamed with the desire to hear this Lord, that she resolved the next day to go to hear him preach. So, when morning came, she got up with great delight in order to go without delay to satisfy her urge, and she dressed herself attentively, as was her habit, for she had considered how to adorn herself so that she might be looked upon favourably and highly esteemed by the great crowd of people who would be attending the sermon. So, leaving her residence on horseback, very well escorted, she arrived at the place where all the people had gathered to listen to Our Lord. And after she had dismounted there, with great difficulty those who were escorting her ensured that space was made so that this lady might be positioned at the front—at which a great hue and cry broke out among the people, who for a long time could not be silenced—leaving her sitting very close to the pulpit so that she could see and hear Our Lord comfortably. And when His Majesty arrived to give his sermon and mounted the platform, he stared at the said Magdalene with those merciful eyes, firing an arrow of love into her heart, while she, feeling herself thus wounded and injured, was completely changed, and her thoughts were transformed.

Our Lord, who had eternally chosen her and realised how great and excellent this lady would turn out to be, addressed his entire sermon to her, speaking of God's great mercies and of how he had come from Heaven in order to reconcile sinners and to secure peace between his eternal Father and them, saying: '*Misericordiam volo et non sacrificium: non enim veni vocare iustos sed peccatores ad paenitentiam*',[2] meaning: 'I wish to grant and to communicate mercy to people, and I wish no other sacrifice than that of heartfelt love, for I have not come to call those who strive to be just, but those who confess and acknowledge themselves to be sinners, and who regret having offended my Father, for this is the true repentance to which I call and invite sinners, namely, that they should recognise their own mistakes and should sincerely abhor them.'

On hearing these things and feeling herself to have been wounded within by the singular grace of divine mercy, while realising that she was already linked and bound by that chain of love, which as time went by grew stronger inside her, the Magdalene lowered her eyes to the ground, placing her fan in front of her face, and started to burst into sobs of tears, saying within her heart: '*Paratum cor meum, Deus!*',[3] meaning: 'O Lord and King of Life, since thus do you want me and draw me towards you with the full power of your bidding, behold, I am ready—and my heart is prepared—to obey you, in that I offer you my entire will, and say to you: "*Domine, quid me vis facere?*",[4] for command, Lord, what you wish me to do and you shall be obeyed unreservedly by me.' And once the sermon was finished, the flame of love having grown inside her, she returned home on foot, no longer wishing to ride, and abhorring in earnest what she had formerly loved so much.

[2] Matthew 9:13.
[3] Psalm 56 [57]:8 [7].
[4] Acts 9:6.

CXVIII

When she arrived home, she quickly entered her most private room and took off all her adornments, casting them on the ground with great distress and abhorrence, recalling how much she had offended her Creator and Lord with those vanities. So, dressed only in a loose gown,[1] with her hair hanging down, this latter being singularly beautiful and long, she threw herself to the ground, with all her weight, saying: '*Cor mundum crea in me, Deus, et spiritum rectum innova in visceribus meis*',[2] meaning: 'O my Lord, you who know how much this heart of mine has been corrupted, wounded and ruined by a multitude of sins and a whole host of vanities, create now, Lord, a new heart within me, so that I see and feel only you, my Life; and that spirit of rectitude attaching to true justice that constitutes your grace, and which I have suppressed and cast out of myself, renew it now, my Lord, within my sorrowful breast.[3] *Quia facere voluntatem tuam, Deus meus, volui, et*

---

[1] Lit. 'gonelle'; Cat. *gonella*. This garment was a long tunic worn by both men and women; the term can also refer to the surcoat worn by knights.

[2] Psalm 50 [51]:12 [10].

[3] Lit. 'heart, innermost being'; Cat. *entràmenes*.

legem tuam in medio cordis mei,[4] for I, Lord, have resolved with all my heart and desire to do your will, and deep within this heart of mine shall be imprinted your law, from which I shall not stray under any conditions. O Lord, let my love, which I have placed so unrestrainedly in temporal things, now be placed entirely in you, so that I neither see nor feel nor love any other than yourself, my Lord, for whom I wish to forsake and abandon all things. *Sed nec inutilis commutatio, pro eo qui super omnia est omnia relinquere, nam et simul cum eo donantur omnia*,[5] for that conversion which consists of renouncing all things in favour of him who is Lord of all things is not futile, but rather highly beneficial, for together with him are all things possessed. O Lord, make me thine, so that I neither desire nor seek nor ask for any other. *Inclinavi cor meum ad faciendas iustificationes tuas propter retributionem*,[6] for I, Lord, have disposed my heart and will to perform and follow your justified counsels and commands for ever, in expectation of reward, which is yourself. *Quoniam apud te est fons vitae, et in lumine tuo videbimus lumen*,[7] for you are the fount of eternal life, and from your light and brightness do we all derive illumination in your kingdom. O Lord, now may I utter the words of David who states: "*Concaluit cor meum intra me, et in meditatione tua exardescit ignis*",[8] for I feel, Lord, that my heart burns within me, and the recollection I have in my mind of your goodness and compassion kindles flames of love in my soul.'

And Our Excellent Magdalene, being thus ardent and inflamed in her love of God, threw off such sparks of true charity that in her was fully confirmed what is written, namely that '*Non potest civitas abscondi supra montem posita*',[9] for since that eminent city called Love—the capital city within the kingdom of the soul, which the omnipotent God has chosen for his dwelling and abode—is one located and founded on that solid mountain which is the heart of that virtuous and kind woman, it is not possible for it to remain concealed, but rather it continuously reveals itself by acts so great and wondrous that they exceed the capacities of men.

[4] Psalm 39 [40]:9 [8].
[5] The first two clauses are found in St Bernard of Clairvaux, *Flores seu Sententiae ex operibus depromptae* (PL 183: 1202B), along with a reference to a pseudo-Augustinian *Tractatulus de contemptu mundi ad clericos*, Chapter 1; the entire sentence, however, occurs in Geoffrey of Clairvaux's ('Bernardi discipulus'), *Declamationes de colloquio Simonis cum Jesu* (PL 184: 438B), a work compiling St Bernard's sermons.
[6] Psalm 118 [119]:112.
[7] Psalm 35 [36]:10 [9].
[8] Psalm 38 [39]:4 [3].
[9] Matthew 5:14.

Such love for God has led women to be resolute in their opposition to tyrants and to emerge invincible from battles with them; to undergo the bitterest torments gladly, while willingly putting themselves forward for any kind of suffering in order to uphold the truth; with the result that today do we sing to the great glory of His Divine Majesty and to the signal honour of the said ladies: '*Deus qui inter cetera potentiae tuae miracula etiam in sexu fragili victoriam martyrii contulisti; qui infirma mundi eligis ut fortia quaeque confundas*',[10] meaning: 'O merciful Lord and God, may boundless thanks be given to Your Royal Majesty, for among the other miraculous acts which proceed from your universal power is the singularly wondrous one of your having granted such resolve to the frail stock of vulnerable women that many of them have died in the victory of glorious martyrdom. And you, Lord, are he who has chosen the frail things of this world, namely women, to instil in them a love of yourself, to the great shame of worldly knights, who have been unable to achieve this.'

And if all women, usually on account of their compassion and kindness, have great privileges, all the more should we believe that Our Excellent Magdalene is exalted and privileged above others, for in love has she surpassed all others. For, after the Most Holy Mother of God, to whom no created being should be compared, the Magdalene felt more love for God than any other woman, and for this reason has Solomon said about her: '*Multae filiae congregaverunt divitias; tu supergressa es universas*',[11] meaning (speaking to the said Magdalene in spirit): 'O glorious Magdalene, even though other women have amassed a great wealth of virtuous deeds, you above all have accumulated those precious coins of the finest gold that are charity and love, which you have invested very wisely by placing it all in the Son of God, *cui angeli serviunt, cuius pulchritudine sol et luna mirantur*,[12] whom the angels serve, and of whose beauty the sun and the moon stand in awe. And therefore do you, O excellent Magdalene, deserve more than all other women to be rewarded, not only in the eternal kingdom where you shall be appropriately glorified, but rather in this present life. While still remaining in your mortal body shall you feel things so lofty and of such sweetness, of the kind you are destined to possess for eternity, that you may quite rightly say: "*Ostendit mihi thesauros incomparabiles, quos mihi se donaturum repromisit*",[13] meaning that you are shown treasures and

---

[10] Two prayers from the divine office.

[11] Proverbs 31:29.

[12] A responsorium from the divine office.

[13] The opening line of a Gregorian chant.

riches beyond compare, which shall be given to you with increase in the land of the living.'[14]

This Magdalene, thus chosen and selected by Our Lord, the Son of God, from among all the women within his dominions in order to be beloved of him to such a degree, and in order that through her he might offer an example of true love to his future servants, let her fervour be shown in many ways, particularly in her great and singular penance, since this is the chief act of love. For it is easy to see that whoever loves deeply is infinitely regretful for having offended his or her beloved; and, therefore, to the Magdalene—being eager to reconcile herself with Our Lord, whom she loved so deeply, and whom she knew she had offended and disobeyed so comprehensively—nothing seemed a hardship in the pursuit of earning his friendship and grace.

[14] *In the land of the living*, i.e. in heavenly glory.

CXIX

THE MAGDALENE, on hearing that Our Lord had been invited to dinner by a Pharisee who lived close to her house, decided to go there to ask
publicly for his mercy, in the presence of everyone, having already
requested it with boundless tears within the privacy of her soul. Even
though she knew that the Pharisee who had issued the invitation was a
great hypocrite and gossip, as well as easily shocked, and that he would not
be pleased to see her in his house, she took no notice of this, thinking only
of pleasing the one whom her soul loved.

So, quite oblivious to her status, and in complete abandonment of
worldly glory, exactly as she stood, in her gown, with her hair loose around
her, she threw a cloak belonging to one of her servant girls over her head
and, all alone, left her house with hurried steps, saying: '*Ambulavit pes meus
iter rectum*',[1] meaning: 'My feet shall move in a straight line until they reach
the presence of the one so beloved by me. *Quem cum tetigero munda sum,*

---

[1] Ecclesiasticus [Sirach] 51:20.

et quis satiabitur videns gloriam eius?,[2] for I firmly believe that as soon as I have come into contact with this infinite good, I shall be cleansed of all my faults. And who can have her fill or tire of seeing the glory and spiritual delight of his presence?' And with this insatiable desire guiding her steps, the loving Magdalene arrived at the house in which lay the treasure she was seeking.

But Our Lord, the Son of God, to whom all things were clear, being aware that this seraphic woman was due to arrive, and wishing to sit down at the table, gave orders to position the chair on which he was to be seated in such a way that he should have his back towards the door of the hall in which the banquet was being held. Accordingly, the Pharisee who had invited him, being seated in front of Our Lord, was facing the door, so that nobody could enter or leave without first being seen by him. So, when the said Magdalene entered through the door of the hall, the said Pharisee, on seeing her, recognised her immediately, even though she had come heavily disguised rather than as she usually looked. He became very perturbed. And frowning, he said to himself: 'What does this woman want in my house?'

So the glorious Magdalene, seeing from behind that Lord whom her soul sought, and becoming completely inflamed with love, said: '*Quemadmodum desiderat cervus ad fontes aquarum, ita desiderat anima mea ad te, Deus*',[3] meaning: 'As a hart longs for spring water, so did my soul long for this sighting of you, who are my Lord and God.' And throwing herself with the most fervent love beneath the table, she embraced those holy and divine feet of Our Lord, her weeping so extreme that all the bones in her body creaked. She kissed his feet many times and, unable to form any words on account of her great floods of tears, said in her heart with a mournful sigh: '*Domine, secundum actum meum noli me iudicare: nihil dignum in conspectu tuo egi; ideo deprecor maiestatem tuam ut tu, Deus, deleas iniquitatem meam*',[4] meaning: 'O my Lord and my Life, please do not judge me according to my acts and deeds, for I confess and acknowledge beyond doubt that I have done nothing worthy of merit nor of reward in the presence of your royal person, but rather endless misdeeds worthy of severe

---

[2] Part of a *responsorium in secundo nocturno*, ostensibly containing the words of St Agnes of Rome, virgin-martyr (*c.*291-*c.*304), sung on her feast day, 21st January, beginning: 'Amo Christum, in cuius thalamum introivi, cuius Mater virgo est ...'; followed by Ecclesiasticus [Sirach] 42:26.

[3] Psalm 41 [42]:2 [1].

[4] A responsorium from the Office for the Dead.

punishment, and therefore, my Lord, I am here to beg Your Majesty to blot out and pardon my iniquities. *Ecce, benignissime Domine, Deus meus, coram te est miseria mea, et in manibus tuis est misericordia tua.* O my most benign Lord and God, look upon me with clement eyes, for in Your Majesty's presence my wretchedness is evident, yet in your compassionate hands lies your mercy. Communicate it to me, my Lord and my Life, for you know *quia misericordia miseris necessaria est*,[5] for the wretched have need of your mercy. O Lord, what wretchedness can be like mine, for I am aware of having offended you infinitely yet I cannot satisfy[6] you in the slightest degree? O Lord, if I, by the torment and suffering of my body, might satisfy the offences committed towards you, how delightful and pleasant in my eyes would such suffering be! No torment exists, Lord, however cruel and painful it might be, that for me would not be a relief if by means thereof I might make reparation for my errors. *Ad te est omne desiderium meum, et gemitus meus a te non est absconditus*;[7] for to you, Lord, is my longing clear, and my sighing is not hidden from you; you alone, who are infinite clemency, know by how much my soul is tormented when I remember that I have offended you and have succumbed to such a multitude of sins. And I am certain *quia stipendia peccati mors*,[8] for the sad wages and payment of sin is death, which is fairly owed to me unless you, my helper, deliver me therefrom by your infinite mercy.

' *Noli abscondere faciem tuam a me; veni in me per gratiam tuam, tange oculos meos spirituales radiis tuae lucis, illustra cor meum lumine tuo, et dic animae meae: salus tua ego sum.*[9] O clement and merciful Lord, do not conceal your sweet face from me on account of my iniquity, but, instead, please come to me by visiting my grieving soul with your grace and mercy, without which I perish. Touch, Lord, my spiritual eyes; let me see within myself the rays of your light; let your light shine in my heart. Tell my soul, Lord, to rejoice, for you are its salvation. *Considera ergo, misericors Deus, naturam infirmitatis meae, et ostende super me magnitudinem bonitatis tuae, quia nemo bonus nisi tu solus.*[10] O Lord, you, who are pure mercy, consider and observe my infirmity and frailty and show unto me the greatness and mag-

[5] St Augustine, *Sermones ad populum. Classis I. De scripturis*, 104.3 (PL 38: 617).

[6] *Satisfy*: in the medieval sense of 'to make (or give) satisfaction' to someone, meaning to 'make amends' or 'compensate' for that person's lost honour.

[7] Psalm 37 [38]:10 [9].

[8] Romans 6:23.

[9] See St Augustine, *Confessiones*, Book I, Chapter 5.5; Ludolph of Saxony, *Vita Jesu Christi*, Part 2, Chapter 24; and cf. Psalm 34 [35]:3.

[10] St Anselm of Canterbury, *Meditatio super Miserere*, 12 (PL 158: 829D).

nitude of your infinite goodness, for nobody is perfectly good apart from
you alone, my Life and my Love! *O quam bonus es, Domine, animae quaerenti te; si quaerenti, quanto magis invenienti.*[11] O merciful Lord, how worthy and profitable it is for the sinful soul to seek and ask for you! And if seeking you, my Lord, is so profitable, how singular and great is the joy of finding you. *Quis per se sine tuo auxilio perfectionis culmen ascendit?*[12] O my Life,
who is it that without your assistance can rise to such perfection as to find
and know you?

'I therefore beg Your Majesty, in these words: *Tu me converte, Deus salu-
taris meus; tu illumina animam meam; tu dirige, tu in me flammam tuae dilec-
tionis accende, ut terram despiciam, caelum aspiciam, peccata odiam, iustitiam
diligam,* [13] for you, Lord, are he who can switch and turn all my affections
to you, who are my salvation, my life and my glory. By you, Lord, may my
soul be guided and enlightened; by you, infinite charity, may the flame of
your love be lit within me.

'So that the world and all sensual things, Lord, be abhorred by me,
may my longing be for Heaven alone and all my love for you, my Lord! May
all kinds of sin be loathsome to me; may the justice of true repentance be
loved by me, and may I be accompanied by such repentance all the days of
my life! With repentance, my Lord, do I wish to forge a close alliance and
friendship, for I am sure it has been stated in its regard that: *Paenitentia
salus animae, restauratio virtutum, despoliatio vitiorum, obtusio inferni, porta
caelorum, via iustorum, refectio bonorum. Felix qui te amat, et te usque ad ulti-
mum vitae suae custodit,* for such virtuous repentance is the salvation and
life of the soul, the restoration of the virtues, the renunciation of the vices,
the wall enclosing Hell, the gateway to the Kingdom of Heaven, the path
taken by those who for every reason wish to get to Paradise, and the revival
of all good; so, therefore, he is called blessed who loves, maintains and preserves it until the very end of his life. And David—of whom you are said to
be a son—who had comprehensive experience of the said virtue, offers
great hope and confidence to sinners, when he says: "*Cor contritum et
humiliatum, Deus, non despicies*",[14] assuring them all that a contrite and
humbled heart is never despised by Your Majesty. O merciful Lord, you

---

[11] St Bernard of Clairvaux, *Sermones de diversis*, 4.1 (PL 183: 552A).

[12] Peter Damian, *Carmina sacra et preces*, I. Oratio ad Deum Patrem (PL 145: 919B).

[13] *Ibid.*, II. Oratio ad Deum Filium (PL 145: 920D); Alcuin, *De psalmorum usu liber*,
39. Oratio sancti Hieronymi pro custodia diei sequentis (PL 101: 490D).

[14] Psalm 50 [51]:19 [17].

know how much my heart grieves and is humbled when I recall that I have
offended you, my Lord and Creator. Do not deny me, Lord, your mercy!
Grant me your forgiveness, for I most sincerely repent my disordered life,
with the firm desire and intention of never offending you or of straying
from obedience to you.'

And while she was uttering these things within her sorrowful and tormented mind, her eyes shed continuous tears, which washed and bathed
the glorious feet of the Son of God. And when the kindly Magdalene saw
the feet of her Lord bathed in such a way by her profuse tears, she kissed
them with infinite love, feeling within herself a singular sweetness which
stirred her to continue her penance, in the greatest assurance of receiving forgiveness from that merciful Lord from whom she had requested it.
And she seemed to hear within her soul that merciful and divine voice saying to her: '*Ego sum qui vocavi te; ego sum qui deleo iniquitates tuas*',[15] meaning: 'Magdalene, take comfort and have full confidence, for I am the one
who has called you and loved you before you came to me, and I am that
true physician whom you seek, and I can heal perfectly the wounds in your
soul and wholly blot out your iniquities.'

So, hearing this voice of mercy within her, she was so happy and joyful
that, with further floods of tears, she said: '*Defecerunt oculi mei in eloquium
tuum dicentes: quando consolaberis me?*',[16] meaning: 'O my Lord and my
Life, as soon as I heard the sweetness of your words my sight began to fail
owing to an abundance of tears, and I said: When shall I attain such complete consolation that my sins might be wholly forgiven and that by your
grace I might be confirmed in your love and close friendship?'

So, kissing those divine feet over and again, she washed them with a
vast outpouring of tears while, using her hair, which was of singular beauty,
she wiped and mopped them with great reverence, wishing to serve him
with that hair by means of which she had offended His Majesty so often. *Ut
totum serviret Deo in paenitentia quicquid ex se Deum contempserat in culpa*,[17]
for she offered every part of herself to the service of God, as continuous
penance, with which parts she knew she had failed to serve him.

And after she had thus washed and wiped the glorious feet of Our
Lord with supreme diligence and indescribable devotion, she embraced
them again with such love that it seemed as if she wished to imprint them

---

[15] An echo of John 4:26; Isaiah 43:25.
[16] Psalm 118 [119]:82.
[17] Gregory the Great, *Homiliarum in evangelia libri duo*, 33.2 (PL 76: 1240B).

upon her soul, and she said with a mournful sigh: '*In te, Domine, speravi: non confundar in aeternum*',[18] meaning: 'O my Lord and my God, in you lies all my hope; let me not eternally be put to shame as my sins warrant; rather I beg Your Majesty, in these words: *Miserere mei, Deus, secundum magnam misericordiam tuam.*[19] O Lord, may it please Your Royal Person to take pity on me in keeping with your customary and time-honoured displays of compassion. *Innova signa et immuta mirabilia,*[20] o merciful Lord, I am sure that the conversion of a sinner is a more difficult and more wondrous matter than the creation of the world, and therefore I beseech Your Majesty to adapt your traditional signs and alter your wondrous deeds, for those great signs which you, my Life, produced when seeking to deliver your chosen people from the captivity of Egypt, you now have to perform spiritually within my soul in order to draw it out from its captivity to the Devil. And the great wonders you carry out each day in healing and raising bodies from the dead, you now have to perform by healing the leprosy of my sinful soul, and by raising it from the cruel death it has incurred.

'I do not ask for physical health; I ask for something greater, and I wish to be more indebted to you than those to whom you have given bodily health. *Quia frustra viveret corporaliter quando spiritualiter in anima moreretur,* for it avails man little to live bodily when his soul spiritually within him is dead. *Quid ergo proderit quia videtur in corpore vivus qui fuerat in anima morte infidelitatis occisus?* And how does seeming to have life in his body benefit the person whose soul has died as a result of faithlessness and disobedience towards his Creator, and who knows that all his deeds are contrary to God's law? This death is the one that ought to be feared and lamented; from this, Lord, do I ask you for resurrection, for I am aware that I have incurred this cruel death on account of my infinite sins, from which you alone are capable of delivering and reviving me, who have stated: "*Ego sum resurrectio et vita; qui credit in me, etiam si mortuus fuerit, vivet*";[21] O Lord, since you are

---

[18] Psalm 70 [71]:1.

[19] Psalm 50 [51]:3 [1].

[20] Ecclesiasticus [Sirach] 36:6.

[21] John 11:25. John 11 contains an account of Jesus' raising of Lazarus (the brother of Mary) from the dead, hence the emphasis in Mary Magdalene's inner address to Jesus on the latter's powers of healing and resuscitation. These details would have been known to the medieval reader. However, in more recent times the Mary (of Bethany) mentioned in John 11:1 has come to be regarded as an entirely distinct figure. Chapters CXXI and CXXII of Isabel de Villena's *Vita Christi* (not included among the present selection) are concerned with Mary Magdalene's relationship with her (ostensive) siblings, Lazarus and Martha.

the resurrection and the life, and you say that all those who believe in you shall not die and that, if they are dead, they shall be resurrected, Lord, with full confidence do I ask you for the life of my soul; grant it to me, Lord, so that I may serve you, love you and know you as my God and Creator and singular benefactor.'

While the Magdalene was saying such things—as well as many others which could not be put into words—within her fervent thoughts, and conversing with her Lord and Master, she repeatedly wiped his divine feet with her own hair, for on account of her continuous tears she would very often bathe them once again as soon as she had wiped them, never tiring of her loving exercise.

So, opening a container she had brought with her, made from a very unique kind of stone, within which there sat a costly oil[22] that she was in the habit of using to preserve her delicate body, and deciding to bring to an end such pleasures and delights and to put everything to use in the service of her beloved, she poured the said oil, thereby anointing and refreshing the tired feet of Our Lord, and considered it to be very well invested in the service of the Creator of all things, who in such hardship and need had trudged across this wretched world for the sake of the salvation of sinners.[23]

[22] Lit. 'a liquor', in the archaic sense of 'grease' or 'oil'. The various biblical accounts all use the word 'ointment'. John's Gospel identifies this ointment as being spikenard.

[23] For this episode, see John 11:2 and John 12:3-8. Cf. Luke 7:36-38.

On how the Pharisee muttered inwardly and how
Our Lord let him know who that singular
lady was [1]

CXX

Shocked, the Pharisee observed this undertaking with revulsion, noting how Our Lord had stopped eating as soon as this woman was beside his feet, appearing to draw greater pleasure from her tears than from the entire banquet feast, and how His Majesty allowed the said woman to touch him and to remain at his feet for such a length of time. So the said Pharisee began to lose the respect he felt for Our Lord and the good opinion he had of him, and, muttering inwardly, said: '*Hic, si esset propheta, sciret utique, quae et qualis est mulier quae tangit eum, quia peccatrix est*',[2] meaning: 'O, if he were as great a prophet as I had thought, he would have known who this woman was as well as the kind of reputation she has, for we all know that she is a great sinner, and even though she may be a woman of rank, whoever does not approve of someone should not show respect to that person, for her reputation does not match her rank, but rather he

---

[1] This chapter and much of the preceding one, with their glosses and mono-logues/dialogues, are structured around the events recounted, and the wording thereof, in Luke 7:36-50.

[2] Luke 7:39. Part of the divine office recited on the Feast of Saint Mary Magdalene.

should cast her out saying: "*Recede longe a me, noli me tangere, quoniam mundus sum*",[3] meaning: "O woman, get away from me, for you are not worthy to touch me, because I am chaste and you are a sinner".'

But Our Lord, to whom all things were clear, seeing this Pharisee sailing thus upon an ocean of conceit, blown by the winds of pride which led him to become so overwrought that he dared to reprimand and judge the works of God without the slightest fear, wished to let him appreciate and understand his ignorance and blindness, by saying: 'Simon—for such was the name of the said Pharisee—I wish to tell you something.' So Simon, feeling extremely annoyed, replied bluntly and curtly, saying: 'Tell me, teacher.'[4]

So Our Lord, paying no heed to his loathsome disdain, said to him very gently: 'Two debtors owed money to a merchant: one owed five hundred shillings,[5] the other fifty, and since they had no means or ability to pay, the merchant forgave them both their entire debt. Which of these two do you think has more of a duty to love the merchant, his benefactor?'

So Simon said in reply: 'In my opinion, I would say that the one to whom more had been given should love much more.'

So Our Lord said to him: 'You have judged rightly. Wait, now, and I shall show you the effects of love, and you shall find out that you possess little thereof and that in you the virtue of charity is sorely lacking, of which virtue it is said: "*Caritas patiens est, benigna est; non irritatur, non cogitat malum; omnia suffert, omnia sperat, omnia sustinet*".[6] For the person who possesses charity is patient and kind; he is not provoked to anger by anybody nor does he take exception; rather, he tolerates all things in order to be of benefit to his neighbour, in the hope that everything will turn out well, and, therefore, he bears willingly any hardship or nuisance for the sake of his neighbour's well-being. And whoever does not find this virtue within him, can truly say: "*Si distribuero in cibos pauperum omnes facultates meas, et si tradidero corpus meum ita ut ardeam, caritatem autem non habuero, nihil mihi prodest*",[7] for alms aplenty are of little avail unless they stem from true charity, and disordered acts of penance should not be deemed wor-

---

[3] Part of the divine office recited on the Feast of St Mary Magdalene: Nocturn 3, Lessons 8 and 9. Cf. Isaiah 65:5 and John 20:17.

[4] Cf. Luke 7:39-50.

[5] The Valencian *sou* (or shilling) consisted of twelve pence. The corresponding text in Luke 7:41 gives 'pence' or 'denarii'.

[6] Cf. 1 Corinthians 13:4-7.

[7] 1 Corinthians 13:3.

thy unless they are accompanied by charity and humility. And have no doubt that *nunquam est Dei amor otiosus*,[8] for God's love is never idle, as I shall show you in practice.'

So, turning round, Our Lord said to Simon: '*Vides hanc mulierem? Intravi in domum tuam: aquam pedibus meis non dedisti; haec autem lacrimis rigavit pedes meos, et capillis suis tersit. Osculum mihi non dedisti; haec autem ex quo intravit, non cessavit osculari pedes meos. Oleo caput meum non unxisti; haec autem unguento unxit pedes meos. Propter quod dico tibi: remittuntur ei peccata multa quoniam dilexit multum*',[9] meaning: 'O Simon, do you see this woman? You despise her for her past sins; I love her for her present deeds, marked by such love and fervour that they deserve to be highly regarded and richly rewarded. For I entered your house and you neglected to provide water for my tired feet in order to give them relief; yet this kind lady —not with ordinary water, but rather with that invaluable sort she has distilled in her own mind by means of the fire of love—has washed and bathed my feet, which she has wiped, not with a silk towel, but rather with her own hair, which she cherished above all things. And you did not greet me with a kiss, as befits charitable love, yet she, as soon as she entered, has not ceased to kiss my feet with profound humility. But you, though you knew how sorely my mind was tired as a result of preaching and praying, have not shown towards me a trace of humanity and compassion by seeking to anoint my head with oil, which is necessary in such cases for the relaxation and relief of an exhausted mind. This humble and courteous woman, on the other hand, not deeming herself worthy to draw near to my head, yet inflamed with love, has anointed my feet with the most costly ointment available, for she considers nothing among her belongings to be fruitfully employed apart from that which is beneficial to my person.

'Therefore, truly I tell you that many sins are forgiven her, for she has loved much, yet it is only right that she be loved. *Cui autem minus dimittitur, minus diligit*:[10] for he who is excused little, loves little. And therefore, since you, Simon, consider that you have been excused little, your love has become so dormant that in none of the said things have you revealed it. *Non quia parum dimittitur, sed quia parum putas esse quod dimittitur.*[11] not because that of which you have been excused is little, but because on account of your conceitedness you consider it to be little.

[8] Gregory the Great, *Homiliarum in evangelia libri duo*, 30.2 (PL 76: 1221D).

[9] Luke 7:44-47.

[10] Luke 7:47.

[11] St Augustine, *Sermones ad populum. Classis I. De Scripturis*, 99.6 (PL 38: 598).

And this is a powerful example of ignorance: namely, that a man should believe himself to have been spared from any kind of sin through his own efforts; for rather, truly I tell you that *nullum est enim peccatum quod fecit homo, quod non possit facere alter homo, si desit rector a quo factus est homo,*[12] for there is no kind of sin which men might have committed to which another man would not sink if he were abandoned and forsaken by that supreme governor and ruler who has made and created man, and therefore no one should despise another however great a sinner he be, for nobody can possess the good all by himself, nor can he preserve it all by himself.

'*O pharisee, si scires quam parum est quod habes, et hoc ipsum quam cito perdis si non servaverit ille qui dedit,*[13] for if only you knew and appreciated, Pharisee, how pitiful is the amount of good that you possess, and how easily you could lose this pitiful amount if it were not preserved by him who has given it to you; whom alone should you thank for the mercies he has shown you in delivering you from the evils you might have committed in accordance with the frailty of your nature, which you have not experienced, and whereby you judge her to be ill, who is healthier than yourself.

'*Quia tu, recumbens quasi sanus, medicum ignoras, quia maiori forsitan febre et mentem etiam perdidisti, nam et frequentius rides ploratus a sanis,*[14] for you sit peacefully, unconcerned by your own illness, yet, considering yourself to be healthy, you ignore the physician, for the fever of conceit is so great that it has led you into an agonising frenzy, and very often you laugh when the healthy, namely, those who know all about your blindness, shed tears for you.

'*Non enim auditores legis iusti apud Deus sunt, sed factores legis iustificabuntur.*[15] Do you not know that nobody is righteous before God by simply hearing the Law being preached unless that person actively fulfils what the Law commands?

'But you follow my sermons, and you praise and endorse them in speech, yet you omit to put them into practice. How can you not recall what I said the other day to a Doctor of the Law who was asking me which was the greatest commandment in the Law? To which I replied: "*Diliges Dominum Deum tuum et proximum tuum sicut te ipsum; in his duobus mandatis*

---

[12] *Idem.*

[13] St Bernard of Clairvaux, *Sermo super psalmum XC, 'Qui habitat',* 1.1 (PL 183: 187B).

[14] St Augustine, *Sermones ad populum, op. cit.,* 99.7 (PL 38: 599).

[15] Romans 2:13.

universa lex pendet et prophetae",[16] affirming that in loving God and one's neighbour lies the complete fulfilment of the Law and of the prophecies.

'So be assured that whoever truly loves God never abhors his creatures, and that whoever loves his neighbour does not disdain sinners, but rather welcomes them with great delight when they come to forgiveness; and whoever fails to observe this should hold and believe that he is the worst of all sinners and has a hidden ailment which is very difficult to cure.

'This woman, whom you have disdained on account of your ignorance, *in brevi explevit tempora multa, et in multitudine electorum habebit laudem, et inter benedictos benedicetur*,[17] for during the brief period she has been at my feet in fervent contrition she has travelled such a great distance that she has arrived at the pinnacle of love's perfection, and has in a short space of time fulfilled the entire Law and its commandments. Therefore, among the great crowd forming the citizens of eternal glory shall she be praised and glorified, and among the number of the blessed shall she be counted and by them uniquely extolled and exalted, for in God has she placed all her faith and hope, and he has taken her into his protection and custody. *Quid enim ei necesse poterit eorum quae sub caelo sunt, quem Deus caeli protegere et conservare voluerit?*[18] Tell me honestly, Pharisee, of all the things that exist beneath the heavens, which is lacking to the person whom God, the Lord of Heaven, takes into his protection and custodianship? In all justice, may it not be said of that person: "*O felix anima quae hanc protectionem meretur*"?,[19] meaning: "O happy soul, who has warranted such protection!"

'And these words can be spoken very truly with regard to this most perfect Magdalene, for with the deepest humility has she confessed her fault, accusing and condemning herself, because of which she deserves to be excused, and to be reconciled with God, and to be protected and diligently guarded by him.'

His Majesty then bringing his conversation with the Pharisee to an end, he directed his words to the said Magdalene, saying to her: '*Remittuntur tibi peccata tua*',[20] meaning: 'O Magdalene, take solace, for the sins for which you have so profusely wept are pardoned and forgiven you.'

Yet some of the guests began to say to themselves: 'Who is this who has

---

[16] Matthew 22:35-40. Cf. Deuteronomy 6:5.

[17] Wisdom (of Solomon) 4:13; Ecclesiasticus [Sirach] 24:4 (Vulgate).

[18] St Bernard of Clairvaux, *Sermo super psalmum XC, 'Qui habitat'*, 1.3 (PL 183: 188B).

[19] *Ibid.*, 1.4 (PL 183: 189A).

[20] Luke 7:48.

so much power to forgive sins?' So Our Lord, seeking to show them that the reflections of each of them were plain and clear to him, said to the Magdalene: '*Fides tua te salvam fecit*',[21] meaning: 'Let no one be astonished at the way you have been pardoned of so many sins, for I say to you assuredly that your faith warrants your having been saved and freed from all guilt. For you have firmly believed that I am able to pardon you, and I am happy to do so, for such a power has been given to me, just as Isaiah states when speaking on my behalf, namely that "*Ego sum ipse qui deleo omnes iniquitates tuas propter me, et peccatorum tuorum non recordabor*".[22] For I am he who can blot out all your iniquities on my own authority, and I do not wish hereafter to recall your sins in order to punish them, for from you I desire no further recompense[23] than your kind and sorrowful tears; by these have you so captivated and conquered me that nothing you request shall be denied. *Vade in pace*,[24] meaning: "Return to your home, for you may be sure that peace has been established between you and me, which peace shall never be sundered." *Quia desponsabo te mihi in fide, pone me ut signaculum super cor tuum*,[25] for I have betrothed you and bound you to me through faith and charity, and I wish you to set me as a seal upon your heart, closing it off from all worldly things; may it be open to me alone, for there do I wish to rest and remain in the absence of any other company.'

So the Magdalene, feeling great happiness, offered in servitude to him her heart and her body, and everything which lay within her, begging him with infinite love to use her house as his home for as long as he stayed in this wretched world.

And Our Lord replied to her: 'Magdalene, I am happy to stay in your house so that it be plain to all how unique is the love I feel towards you. And the Magdalene, bidding farewell to His Majesty, said with untold joy: '*Quis deus similis tui, qui aufers iniquitatem et transfers peccatum? Quoniam non est confusio confidentibus in te*',[26] meaning: 'O my Lord and my Life, which god is like you, who pardons and forgives iniquities and takes away the sins of the soul which approaches you? O Lord, it is certainly very true that he cannot be shamed who puts his trust in you!'

---

[21] Luke 7:50.
[22] Isaiah 43:25.
[23] Lit. 'satisfaction'.
[24] Luke 7:50.
[25] Hosea 2:20 (Vulgate); Song of Solomon 8:6.
[26] Micah 7:18; Daniel 3:40.

CXXIV

SO, CONTINUING his preaching, Our Merciful Lord passed through
that Land of Judaea and of Galilee with the greatest of toil. And on one
occasion, on his way through Samaria, which was a land of unbelievers, His
Majesty came to a city called Sychar,[2] and there outside the city was that
fine well built by Jacob, which he left by inheritance to his son Joseph.

And approaching the said well, Our Lord leant against its edge,
appearing to be very tired and inconvenienced by the journey. *Non enim
frustra fatigatur Iesus; non enim frustra fatigatur virtus Dei; non enim frustra
fatigatur per quem fatigati recreantur,*[3] for we may be completely sure that it
was not without good reason that Our Lord Jesus seemed exhausted—he
who is the divine power by which all those who are tired or exhausted find
themselves revived,[4] since when he is present by grace nobody feels tired,
yet when he withdraws, man then feels the frailty of his wretched nature.

---

[1] John 4:4 ff.
[2] Also known as Shechem.
[3] St Augustine, *In evangelium Joannis tractatus CXXIV*, 15.6 (PL 35: 1512).
[4] Cat. *recreats*, also having the more technical sense of 'redeemed' (see below also).

Our Lord wished men to understand and to realise that he is both strong and weak. His strength is acknowledged when it is said of His Majesty that '*In principio erat Verbum, et Verbum erat apud Deum, et Deus erat Verbum*',[5] for the Son of God is without beginning and without end, and equal to his Father. '*Omnia per ipsum facta sunt, et sine ipso factum est nihil, et sine labore facta sunt*',[6] for through his power are all things created and made, and without him can nothing be made, and without any toil are his works performed. What kind of strength can be like that of His Majesty who does all things without toil, by command alone? And his weakness is revealed when it is said of him that '*Et Verbum caro factum est et habitavit in nobis*',[7] for men shall be in a position to say: 'That Son of God so potent was made man in order to dwell and abide among us so that he who, through his power, has created us might, in his humility and weakness, revive and strengthen us; for his strength has brought into being those things which did not exist, and his weakness preserves those which did so that they should not perish. For this reason did he seem to be sick, so that he might heal the sick, and his weakness resided in the human flesh assumed by him, in which flesh His Majesty experienced infinite toil and suffering.'[8]

While Our Lord was resting thus at the said well, his disciples entered the city in order to acquire something they might eat for lunch. While Our Lord was by himself, there came a Samaritan woman to draw water from that well, and Our Lord, observing her with a gracious expression, said to her: '*Da mihi bibere*',[9] meaning: 'Woman, when you have drawn water, give me some of it, for I am weary with thirst.' So the said woman, beholding His Majesty, and seeing that he wore the clothing of a Jew, said to him: 'I am amazed at you, since you are a Jew and you ask me for water, who am a Samaritan woman. Are you Jews not all so aloof and disdainful of Samaritans, that you won't even speak to or communicate with them?'

So, in answer to her, Our Lord said: '*Si scires donum Dei, et quis est qui dicit tibi: da mihi bibere, tu forsitan petisses ab eo, et dedisset tibi aquam*

---

[5] John 1:1.
[6] John 1:3.
[7] John 1:14.
[8] An oblique reference to St Gregory of Nazianzen's dictum (against the Apollinarian heresy): 'What has not been assumed has not been healed', asserting that Christ has a complete human nature, body and soul, upon which the redemptive aspect of the Incarnation rests. This passage, therefore, emphasises the passible features of Christ's humanity, an emphasis common among Franciscan writers, of which Isabel de Villena forms a part, as a Poor Clare.
[9] John 4:7.

vivam',[10] meaning: 'O woman, if you only knew the full degree of the grace that you have found today, inasmuch as the Son of God asks tidings of you and desires your salvation! O if you knew who it is that is speaking to you and asking for a drink, how eagerly would you ask him to give you living water!'

Thereafter, the Samaritan woman, already fully inflamed with love for Our Lord, began to speak to him with greater reverence—for love brings reverence and fear—saying to him: 'But, Sir, you have nothing with which to draw water, and the well is very deep. From where will you manage to obtain that living water you mention? Do you, Sir, outshine our great father Jacob, who gave this well to us, from which he drank himself, as did his sons and all his livestock?'

In reply, Our Lord said to her: '*Omnis qui biberit ex aqua hac, sitiet iterum; qui autem biberit ex aqua quam ego dabo ei, non sitiet in aeternum,*[11] for be assured that all those who drink of this water from the well before us will thirst again, whereas those who drink of the water that I shall give them will never thirst; *sed aqua quam ego dabo ei fiet in eo fons aquae salientis in vitam aeternam,*[12] rather, this water that I give will produce in those who drink it a spring of water welling up to eternal life. In other words, charity and grace so enliven the soul in which they reside, that they make it well upwards through continuous contemplation of and longing for eternal life.'

But the simple-minded Samaritan woman, failing to understand Jesus's words on account of her inexperience in spiritual matters, and seeing everything in terms of bodily pleasure and repose, said to His Majesty: 'Sir, please give me some of this water, that I may thirst no more nor have to come here to draw from the well, for it exhausts me to come here every day.'

Our Lord, therefore, realising that this woman understood only worldly things, said to her: 'Go, call your husband.'

And the woman replied to him, saying: 'I have no husband.'

So Our Lord said to her: 'Given the circumstances, I'm pleased that you've told the truth, for you have had five husbands yet the one you are with now is not your husband, and therefore you have spoken well, and admitted the truth, by saying that you have no husband.'

On hearing this, the said woman was completely astonished and amazed, and said: 'Sir, it would seem that you are a prophet and know every-

---

[10] John 4:10.
[11] John 4:13-14.
[12] John 4:14.

thing; I suspect, then, that you can tell me my hidden sins. If you are willing, let us change the subject, for the truth is disagreeable to hear. May it please you, Sir, to resolve a doubt I have, namely the following: our ancestors worshipped and prayed on this mountain called Gerizim,[13] yet you Jews state that Jerusalem is the true place for prayer and that Our Lord God ought to be worshipped there. Tell me, Lord, which opinion is truer and more sure, so that I may follow that one, for it seems to me that you are a wise man, and I shall consider your conclusion to be completely beyond doubt.'

Our Lord, noting the virtuous desire of this woman, who wished to be informed of the most appropriate place to offer prayer, said to her: '*Mulier, crede mihi, quia venit hora quando neque in monte hoc neque in Hierosolymis adorabitis Patrem*',[14] meaning: 'Woman, since you have so much faith in me, I wish to tell you the truth, for you can be sure that the hour is coming—namely, when the Law of the Gospels is made known—in which neither on this mountain nor in Jerusalem will you worship the Father. *Vos adoratis quod nescitis, nos adoramus quod scimus, quia salus ex iudaeis est*,[15] for you worship what you do not know, whereas we Jews proceed according to the Law, and we know and are convinced that salvation is promised to us. *Sed venit hora, et nunc est, quando veri adoratores adorabunt in spiritu et veritate. Nam et Pater tales quaerit qui adorent eum. Spiritus est Deus, et eos qui adorant eum, in spiritu et veritate oportet adorare.*[16] Certainly, the hour is coming, and has already arrived, when the devout and true worshippers shall offer their prayer in spirit and in true sincerity; in other words, their hearts shall agree with their speech and their deeds shall not differ from their words. And such does the eternal Father wish those to be who offer true and pleasing worship to him. For God is spirit, and it is necessary that the spirit of those who seek fittingly to worship His Majesty should be truly purified, and, this being so, any place is suitable for praying. David said, therefore, speaking to his soul: "*In omni loco dominationis eius, benedic, anima mea, Domino*",[17] meaning: "O my soul, all places on earth are under the lordship and dominion of Our Lord God; in every one of them can you praise and worship His Majesty, and you need not climb a mountain in order to be closer to Heaven and to Our Lord God." *Quia qui in altis*

----

[13] Mount Gerizim, 25 miles (40 km) north of Jerusalem, is close to Sychar (Shechem).

[14] John 4:21.

[15] John 4:22.

[16] John 4:23-24.

[17] Psalm 102 [103]:22.

habitat humilibus apropinquat,[18] for be assured that he who dwells and abides in the heavenly heights draws near to the humble. And of such says David: "*Ascensiones in corde suo disposuit, in valle lacrimarum*",[19] for in the deep valley of humility tears are never absent, yet man, descending into the said valley out of awareness of his own sins, lays the firm foundations of the ladder by which to ascend and to experience the divine comforts, and the more frequently he descends, the more ascents he makes ready in his heart. And, therefore, be assured that all those who seek to ascend in my grace and love have first to descend into an awareness of their wretchedness, and to say in their hearts as well as their speech: "*Iniquitatem meam ego cognosco, et peccatum meum contra me est semper.*"[20] For whoever is aware of his iniquity and wretchedness, holds his sins continually before him, sins which reprimand and reproach him, so that pride and vanity are not capable of affecting him, nor do they give him licence to disdain anyone.'

When the Samaritan woman had heard these words of Our Lord, a great devotion towards him was kindled and inflamed in her, and she said to him: 'O Lord, how satisfied and contented I am by your sweet words, though they be very obscure to me, who am an ignorant woman. One thing I've heard said, however, makes me happy, namely that the Messiah is coming, and when he has arrived, he will show us all things and will enlighten our intellects so that we know his ways, and we shall proceed along them, for it is said of him that just as a mother loves and nurtures her children, so too will he love us, and therefore I desire to see him, that I may love and serve him, and follow in his footsteps.'

So Our Lord, the Son of God, who rejoices in the desires of the humble, replied to the devout Samaritan woman, saying: 'O woman, you are familiar with the common adage: "God brings about a desire that's devout." *Ego dabo tibi thesaurus absconditos et arcana secretorum, ut scias quia ego Dominus,*[21] for be assured that I wish to give you that great and hidden treasure of my grace and to communicate to you that hiddenmost secret of human redemption, and I wish you to know and to realise from conclusive experience that I am the Lord and true Messiah you so desire. Here am I speaking to you, and communicating to you who I am and the reason why I have come; for you are here as the representative of all women, to

[18] St Thomas Aquinas, *Catena aurea in quatuor evangelia. Expositio in Ioannem*, Chapter 4, Lesson 4.
[19] Psalm 83:6-7 (Vulgate).
[20] Psalm 50 [51]:4.
[21] Isaiah 45:3.

whom I wish to give this singular glory, so that to them alone through special love should I have said and openly explained, speaking to you as their representative: "*Ego sum, qui loquor tecum*",[22] for I, who speak to you, am the one you seek.'

So the kindly woman, having learnt that he was the true Messiah, sought to communicate the treasure she had discovered to her neighbours, being magnanimous and in no way miserly. Leaving behind her pitcher and her rope, she ran to the city, telling the men of that place: 'Come quickly and you shall see a divine man, who has told me everything I keep hidden about my life, and be sure that he is Christ, that is, the true Messiah.'

On hearing this, the said men, dropping everything, emerged with great delight to welcome Our Lord, who out of mercy was coming to visit them.

However, his disciples had returned with the food before these people had arrived, although Our Lord did not wish to eat, since he was waiting for those who were coming, so he said to his disciples who were begging him to eat: '*Meus cibus est ut faciam voluntatem eius qui misit me*',[23] meaning: 'Be assured, my disciples, that my delicious food lies in doing the will of my Father, who has sent me to convert souls and to draw them towards him.'

So, the people now having arrived, they found His Majesty near the well conversing with his disciples, and Our Lord welcomed them most lovingly, informing them at length about the salvation of souls; and they, very contented and satisfied by his words, begged His Majesty to stay with them. So, in order to make them happy, Our Lord remained there for two days, letting them and those yet to come know that through the observance of two commandments would they be saved and achieve the repose of Paradise.

[22] John 4:26.
[23] John 4:34.

CXXV

AFTER OUR LORD had left that people of Samaria, he continued to preach the Gospel. Travelling on foot, and with infinite difficulty he went around the world. And, at one point, while he was travelling in the areas of Tyre and Sidon, a Canaanite woman who had heard that he was coming—an unbeliever, outside the Judaic law—and whose house lay in the vicinity, found herself in great distress and anguish. Yet knowing the great reputation of Our Lord, she decided to introduce herself to him and to ask him if he would relieve her suffering, for she had a daughter, whom she loved dearly, who was possessed by a wicked demon.

So, emerging from her house, the said Canaanite woman, with great heartache and distress, left her daughter alone inside, locking the door with a key, and hurried along the road upon which Our Lord was travelling in the company of a crowd of people.

So the said woman, seeing His Majesty from afar, began to let out great cries in order to make known her distress, saying: 'Miserere mei, Domine, fili David!',[2] meaning: 'O son of a merciful father, have pity on my suffering!

---

[1] The account given here is based on Matthew 15:21-28.
[2] Matthew 15:22.

Filia mea male a daemonio vexatur,[3] for my daughter is tormented in her body and I in my soul. She emerged from my innards, and there do I feel the sharp pain of her suffering, and feel that pain as my own. Therefore, Sir, I ask you to have mercy on me, for by healing my beloved daughter you shall remove my suffering, for while she is unwell I am unable to achieve repose for an hour or even a minute. O Lord, your father David, who was so merciful, pardoned his enemy and spared the life of him who wished to spill his blood! I do not ask as much, Lord: I simply implore you to deliver my daughter from your enemy, for he torments her by means of cruel pains within her body. *Non enim de foris venit, sed intus est expugnator; in se habet hostem et gladium; navis est quae de se concitat tempestatem; non invenio nomen passionis eius*, for her suffering and tribulation comes not from without nor visibly: inside her lies her assailant; within herself does she bear her persecutor and his knife. O Lord, what ship is this that all by itself arouses the storm and the tempest! I find no suitable name by which to call the cruel illness and affliction of my dear daughter! I have no remedy for my distress other than to call on you, o fount of mercy, with the words: '*Miserere mei, Domine, fili David!*'[4]

So Our Lord, who knew the great resolve of this woman, wished her patience to be confirmed and widely known, and therefore he let her cry out loud, and did not turn to her or say anything to her, but indicated instead that he did not wish to listen to her. So His Majesty entered a house and ordered the door to be shut.

Then the said Canaanite woman, completely untroubled by his disdain, and with the most fervent faith, approached the door, and knocking hard she said: 'O Lord, so you cast me off and reject me! This wooden door you have closed on me, yet that of your heart you have opened to me, for you are the one who overcomes and who heals as much as you please! I, Lord, shall not tire, since I know for sure that you have said: "*Pulsate, et aperietur vobis; petite, et dabitur vobis; quaerite, et invenietis*",[5] commanding me to knock with great confidence, for you, Lord, shall open this door to me, and thus I shall never leave here until I am entitled to see you in the flesh, and I shall ask constantly until you see fit to grant my request, and I shall not refrain from seeking your mercy until you render me worthy of finding it.

[3] *Idem.*
[4] *Idem.*
[5] Matthew 7:7.

'O kind Lord, open this irksome door which prevents me from seeing your divine face! Look at me, Sir, with eyes of mercy, for sorrow makes me cry aloud and love won't let me rest! Need compels me to ask. Set me free, Lord, that I may return to my daughter, who torments my soul! My heart is riven: the greater part remains with my tormented daughter, the lesser with me. For never have I left her or ever forsaken her for a single hour until now, in order to come to you to ask for her salvation, and I shall not refrain from crying aloud, since I follow the counsel of Isaiah, who states: "*Clama, ne cesses, quasi tuba exalta vocem tuam, et sanitas tua citius orietur, quia misericors est Dominus Deus tuus*",[6] since, even if my bodily strength fails me, the pain in my heart shall make me cry out all the louder in the hope of obtaining that salvation so greatly desired. For I am convinced that you, my Lord and God, are infinitely merciful and kind, and you do not refuse those who seek you if they ask you at the proper time. And thus does Isaiah make the same claim: "*Quaerite Dominum dum inveniri potest, invocate eum dum prope est*",[7] encouraging sinners to seek you now that they can find you, for when you dwelt in the heights of Heaven nobody could go to you to ask for mercy, nor did sinners presume to have such audacity, for they knew that it was written: "*Longe a peccatoribus salus, quia eos Deus non audit*",[8] for salvation and eternal life was very remote and far away from sinners, and by you, merciful Lord, they were not heard. But now that you have decided to come down to earth clad in our own flesh, it is time for us to seek you and to ask your forgiveness, for you are so close that we can say to each other: "*Ecce nunc tempus acceptabile, ecce nunc dies salutis*",[9] meaning: "Behold, the acceptable time has come, as has the day of salvation on which man may speak and converse with his Lord and God." *Ideo descendisti, ideo carnem suscepisti ut ego loquar ad te et cum fiducia petam*,[10] for to this end, Lord, did you come down and have you taken on human flesh, so that I might dare to talk to you and with great confidence and audacity ask and say: *Miserere mei, Domine, fili David!*[11]

---

[6] A conflation of Isaiah 58:1; 58:8 and Deuteronomy 4:31.

[7] Isaiah 55:6.

[8] A conflation of Psalm 118 [119]:155 and John 9:31.

[9] 2 Corinthians 6:2.

[10] Reputedly the words of Laurentius (*fl.* 5th-6th century), one-time Bishop of Novara and later Milan, with regard to the Canaanite woman. See P. Allix, *Some Remarks upon the Ecclesiastical History of the Ancient Churches of Piedmont*, Oxford, Clarendon Press, 1821, Chapter 5, p. 29.

[11] Matthew 15:22.

But Our Lord, delighting in the great constancy and resolve of this wise woman, wished to test her patience even further, so he ordered the doors of the house to be opened, seeking to depart therefrom, and he went on his way in a great hurry, saying not a word to the Canaanite woman nor making mention of her. Yet the woman, completely unaffected by the disdain which had been shown her, lifted herself up with a more fervent resolve, following Our Lord, and continuing her calls requesting mercy. She then approached the disciples, first one, then the other, grasping hold of them with great fervour of spirit, and saying: 'O blessed are you, who are deemed worthy to accompany and follow this Lord! Be my intercessors, and beg him to have pity on my suffering, for I am convinced that it lies in his power to put a stop to my pain! And you, who are so intimate with this king of mercy and compassion, obtain this grace for me, that I may not die of thirst before the living fount of infinite sweetness!'

So the kind Apostles, with tears running down their faces, knelt in front of their Lord and Master, and begged His Majesty, saying: '*Dimitte eam, quia clamat post nos*',[12] meaning: 'O Lord, may you set this woman free by giving her what she asks, for there exists no heart that is not rent by having seen and heard her suffering and her pitiful tears! O Lord, such a just cause demands that her daughter be healed! Why do you make her suffer so? You, Lord, who are so quick to employ mercy, why do you forget your custom and do something as unexpected as to deny the person who asks you? Utter, Lord, some word of comfort to her, for you already know that women are most loving, and that since they love, they wish to be loved, and they experience great sorrow if they encounter the opposite. And this Canaanite woman, freshly converted, has persevered with such faith and love in asking from you something so easy to accomplish, yet the fact that she has not heard a single pleasant word from Your Majesty is something which causes her much pain and suffering. *Ubi sunt misericordiae tuae antiquae, Domine?*[13] Where, Lord, are your customary mercies of old, which have not been shown towards this woman?'

So Our Lord, the Son of God, replied to his Apostles, saying: 'Consider this, my disciples: *Non sum missus nisi ad oves, quae perierunt domus Israel,*[14] I was primarily sent only to the sheep who perish from the House of Israel, yet you wish me to perform a miracle upon this woman, an unbeliever, who stands outside the Judaic law!'

[12] Matthew 15:23.
[13] Psalm 88:50 (Vulgate).
[14] Matthew 15:24.

CXXVI

So THE SAID Canaanite woman, who heard that Our Lord was giving an account of his task to the Apostles, was very happy, and strengthening her resolve, she passed through the entire crowd of people, and arriving in front of His Majesty, Our Lord, the Son of God, she threw herself at his feet with such a sorrowful cry that it seemed as if her heart would burst, saying: '*Domine, adiuva me*', meaning: 'O help me, my Lord, who alone are able to help me! *Quia ad tuam misericordiam confugio,*[1] for I have come for your mercy. This is my refuge and my hope: namely, that for this reason, Lord, have you come into the world, in order to show your compassion towards sinners; for, even though I believe you to be the almighty God and in this respect I tremble before your divine presence, when I see that you are a man, I acquire the boldness to speak to Your Majesty. *Cherubim aspectum tuum tremunt in caelo, et ego, mulier in terra, cum fiducia accedo ad te; angeli metuunt in excelsis, et ego, peccatrix, loquor tecum.* I am certain that the Cherubim, in Heaven, tremble before your presence and venerate and obey it, while I, a wretched little woman, on earth, with great confidence

---

[1] St Anselm of Canterbury, *Meditatio super Miserere*, 1 (PL 158: 821B).

dare to approach you, kind Lord; and the holy angels fear you in the heights of your supreme kingdom, while I, a sinner, dare to speak with you, constantly asking for your mercy, without pause. For your disciples have greatly consoled and comforted me in my tribulations by telling me not to grow weary, since to those who persevere is given that for which they ask.

'And the greatest of them, the one who walks at your side, and is called Peter, I think, said to me: "*Non est enim apud Deum personarum acceptio, non rex apud illum nobilior, non pauper infirmior*",[2] meaning that in your presence nobody is shown preference, for a king is not more noble nor more greatly respected by Your Majesty than a pauper so long as they do not differ in virtue, for in your Court no other rank is mentioned.

'And your first cousin, John, appropriately beloved above all others, whispered in my ear: "*Deus caritas est, et qui manet in caritate in Deo manet, et Deus in eo*",[3] meaning that you, Lord, are charity—or love—itself, and that, if I seek to possess you, I must have this virtue in me, and in that case you, Lord, shall abide in me and I in you. So, hereafter, my Life, shall I do what you command, while you, merciful Lord, shall give to me what I ask from you, for my faith is steadfast and subject to no change.

'And James, your other first cousin, said to me: "*Postulet autem in fide nihil haesitans*",[4] for if I ask with steadfast faith, nothing shall be denied me. Who, Lord, having such witnesses and by you so endorsed, can be faithless enough to doubt, for I am more than certain that what they have said, they have heard entirely from your lips? *Ipsos etiam intercessores habere merear:* because for me it shall be a singular grace, through their intercession, to deserve to obtain clemency from you. O merciful Lord, listen to them if I am not worthy of being heard, and for the sake of the worthy have pity on me, who am unworthy!'

So then Our Lord replied to her, saying: '*Non est bonum sumere panem filiorum et mittere canibus*',[5] meaning: 'O woman, do you not know that it is not fair to take the children's bread and give it to the dogs?'

---

[2] Partial citation in St Thomas Aquinas, *Catena aurea in quatuor evangelia. Expositio in Lucam*, Chapter 18, Lesson 1. The entire sentence appears in a *Sermo Reverendi Magistri Marci Berga praestantissimus, die exequiarum dicti domini regis factus*, edited by Petrus Michael Carbonellus (Pere Miquel Carbonell, the Catalan historian and humanist, 1434-1517) in *De exequis, sepultura et infirmitate regis Joannis secundi*, Chapter 71; see M. de Bofarull i de Sartorio (ed.), *Colección de Documentos Inéditos del Archivo de la Corona de Aragón*, 27, Barcelona, 1864, pp. 242-251, quotation on p. 246.

[3] 1 John 4:16.

[4] James 1:6.

[5] Matthew 15:26.

Yet the most fervent woman, replying with profound humility, said:
'O Lord, what you say is very true! I am not so ignorant that I seek to equate
myself with the Jews, who, because they are your children, are my masters,
nor do I ask you to perform for me the great miracles you have performed
and continue to perform every day among them. *Nam et catelli edunt de
micis quae cadunt de mensa dominorum suorum.*[6] But, as you know, Lord, the
whelps eat and survive on the crumbs that fall from their masters' table,
and if I am not deserving of an entire loaf as a daughter, let me have a single crumb as a whelp. That, Sir, will sate me and leave me satisfied.
I seek but one word from you: that you command my daughter to be
healed.'

So Our Lord, the Son of God, who sincerely loves the humble,
observing the great constancy and humility of this woman, and seeking
to praise and glorify her in the presence of that great crowd of people
which was following him, said to her: '*O mulier, magna est fides tua: fiat
tibi sicut vis*',[7] meaning: 'O woman, you are worthy of great praise and
renown, for deeply have you loved and firmly believed, whereby you
deserve to be given what you request in abundance. So, let it be done just
as you wish so that it be clear to all how much I bind myself to those who
love me, for, despite the fact that at the beginning I may constrain myself
a little, later I give them much more than they request, and I satisfy and
gratify their wishes and desires more completely than they know how to
ask.'

So the Canaanite woman, seeing the great gentleness and magnificence of Our Lord, who spoke to her with such love in granting her the
return to health, so greatly desired, of her dear daughter, turned her tears
of sorrow into extraordinary joy, and thanked His Majesty for his bounti-
ful mercy, throwing herself at his feet and saying: 'O merciful Lord, that
close confidant and first cousin of yours, the glorious John, most certainly
told me the truth when comforting me in my distress. Encouraging me to
continue with my pleas, he said to me: "*Fiduciam habemus ad Dominum, et
quodcumque petierimus ab eo accipiemus*",[8] meaning that nobody who has
full trust in you shall ever be denied the grace for which he asks. Thus,
Lord, as I now realise from experience in my own case, with little effort
have I achieved a great recovery in terms of my anguish and salvation as

[6] Matthew 15:27.
[7] Matthew 15:28.
[8] 1 John 3:21-22.

regards my daughter, whom I consider to have been healed already, since you have ordered it be done just as I wished, and to Your Majesty it is clear that, more than my own well-being, I have desired that of this daughter so beloved to me. Now that I have achieved this through you, I am freed from all suffering, and with your permission, I shall return to that daughter whom, with such distress, I left behind.'

After the Canaanite woman had bade farewell to Our Lord, she arrived home to find her daughter healed. So the two of them embraced each other in floods of tears, offering thanks to divine mercy, which had given them such contentment and repose, remaining deeply stirred to serve His Majesty throughout all the days of their lives.

ON HOW, WHILE OUR LORD WAS IN THE TEMPLE, A WOMAN
TAKEN IN SIN WAS INTRODUCED TO HIM BY THE PHARISEES
AND ON HOW HE SAVED HER FROM DEATH[1]

CXXVIII

AFTER OUR LORD, the Son of God, had preached for a while in Galilee,
he departed therefrom and returned to Jerusalem, where he found the
ill will of the Pharisees already so aroused against him that these men
caused him infinite suffering and persecution, disguising their envy
with great zeal for justice, seeking novel and wily forms of malevolence
with which they could slander him and cause the people to think ill of him.
And the extinguished fire that was the Pharisees' hypocritical and cun-
ning vindictiveness smouldered all the while without making a flame.

So one day while Our Lord was sitting in the temple and all the
people were coming up to him with great devotion in order to hear his
divine words, and he was most lovingly informing them about the Law of
the Gospel, telling them at length about the great and infinite mercies of
his divine Father, the people, immensely stirred by the sweetness of his

---

[1] This chapter is based on the account given in John 8.

words, said to him: '*Diffusa est gratia in labiis tuis, propterea benedixit te Deus in aeternum*',[2] meaning: 'O Lord, so much grace spills from your lips! And thus do they know that Our Lord has blessed you for eternity!'

But the said Pharisees, who were observing and listening to this with great indignation, sought to catch Our Lord out and to put him to shame in the presence of all those people, so they brought before him a woman who had been taken in sin and, placing her in the midst of all the people in front of His Majesty, said to him: 'Master, this woman has just been found in adultery and, according to the law, Moses urges and commands that she be stoned, yet just now you were talking at such length about mercy that we should like to know your thoughts as to what should be done with this woman, for we have all decided to abide by your ruling, since we are sure that you will only speak the truth.'

They did all this in the belief that on whichever side he answered, he could only err. O Pharisees, dissembling hypocrites, it is of you that David spoke when he said: '*Molliti sunt sermones eius super oleum, et ipsi sunt iacula*',[3] meaning that the words of the Pharisees in the past and of hypocrites in the present are smoother than any butter,[4] yet, in conjunction with such words, and without the slightest mercy, these men fire arrows dipped in mortal venom. *Quia per suos dulces sermones seducunt corda innocentium*:[5] for with their sweetened and dissembling words they deceive and beguile the hearts of innocent men.

So Our Lord, having seen the malevolence of those people, considered them carefully though said nothing to them. Instead, he stooped down, bending towards the ground, and wrote in the dust with his own finger the following words: '*Qui de terra est de terra loquitur*',[6] meaning: 'O Pharisees, just as you are worldly and sinful, so you speak only of sins, yet these do you proceed to seek out and to inquire after, not from a desire for the salvation of souls, but so as to put into effect your vindictiveness!'

But the said Pharisees, not knowing what he had written, were in a great hurry for him to answer their question and to tell them his opinion. So Our Lord, lifting himself up, said to them: '*Qui sine peccato est vestrum, primus in illam lapidem mittat*',[7] meaning: 'My opinion on this matter is the

---

[2] Antiphon used on the Feast of St Lucy, 15th December.
[3] Psalm 54 [55]:22 [21].
[4] Lit. 'liquor of oil'.
[5] Romans 16:18.
[6] John 3:31.
[7] John 8:7.

following, namely, that if this woman must be stoned, then the first stone should be cast at her by the hand of him among you that is without sin, for, otherwise, an injustice would be done to her if by sinners her sin were chastised.'

So, having said this, he bent down to the ground once more and wrote the words: '*Terra, terram accusas?*',[8] meaning: 'O you, who are all worldly on account of the great envy which has control of you, and which does not let you consider or be concerned with anything apart from the world and the things therein! How can you accuse this woman, who, having followed her worldly and sensual inclinations, has committed a sin, when you are guilty of infinitely many sins that are worse and of a more grievous kind, for in your souls have they grown deep-rooted yet remained un-acknowledged?'

But when the said Pharisees looked on the ground at the words Our Lord, the Son of God, had written, they became fully aware, within their consciences, of the great evils and iniquities that they had committed throughout the entirety of their wrongful lives. So, ashamed and embarrassed, yet not at all reformed, they departed from there, being unable to stand their ground or to give any account of themselves, or for any one of them to wait for the others, since each took flight in his own direction, having neither the resolve nor the ability to persist in the accusation they had hypocritically begun. So, therefore, of men such as these is it said: '*Vir duplex animo inconstans est in omnibus viis suis*',[9] for a double-faced and dissembling person lacks steadfastness and constancy in all he does. And those who began to flee first of all were the eldest, for it is written: '*Qui maior est aetate, maior est iniquitate*',[10] for he who lives wrongfully, increases in iniquity the older he grows.

So, once these malicious Pharisees had left, Our Lord remained alone, abandoned by that disagreeable company, for those who stayed with him were the Apostles and the devout people, who were in such conformity with his will and so obedient to him that they could be called a single will. And it is written, therefore, that His Majesty was left alone, for whoever abides in agreeable company can say that he is alone with himself, and

---

[8] Cf. Jeremiah 22:29; John 8:6-8. The very words Jesus wrote, as here specified, appeared in the tenth-century *Codex Egberti* (Trier, Stadtbibliothek, MS 24), though had been the focus of speculation since the times of St Ambrose (*c.*337/340-397) and St Augustine (354-430).

[9] James 1:8.

[10] St Augustine, *Sermones ad populum, op. cit.,* 115.4 (PL 38: 657).

whoever finds himself with people who are at odds with his own will, must reckon that he is accompanied by a crowd of people, and can say: '*Multiplicasti gentem et non magnificasti laetitiam*',[11] for from such multiplication of company there does not follow joy or happiness, but rather continuous tribulation.

But the accused woman having remained there among them, abandoned by her cruel accusers, yet acknowledging her guilt and feeling remorseful about it, awaited with great fear what her sentence might be. And, ashamed and greatly embarrassed at her error, she did not dare raise her eyes or speak a single word; within her heart alone was she riven by sorrowful moans, desiring to obtain mercy from that kindly judge to whom she had been introduced.

So Our Merciful Lord, seeing her thus distressed and trembling all over, moved by great compassion, said to her: '*Mulier, ubi sunt qui te accusabant? Nemo te condemnavit?*',[12] meaning: 'O woman, where are your accusers? Has none of them condemned you?' And the woman, very joyful, seeing that Our Lord had spoken to her with such gentleness, replied to him: '*Nemo, Domine*',[13] meaning: 'If you, Lord, are with me, no accuser can harm me. *Nam, etsi ambulavero in medio umbrae mortis, non timebo mala, quoniam tu mecum es*,[14] for if I, Lord, were brought to the point of death, as my sins warrant, and were then to feel the anguish of that shadowy hour, I should fear no evil since I would experience your favour and your aid.'

So Our Lord, to whom all these things were clear, realised the great fear and terror that this woman had in her heart, given that she was highly apprehensive as to what would become of her, since she knew that the law was against her unless His Majesty, who was above that law and could make exemptions therefrom, were to help her. Moved by great compassion, therefore, and wishing to give her assurances as regards her life, he said to her: '*Nec ego condemnabo te*',[15] meaning: 'You already know quite how well-disposed I am towards women, because I am aware that they are loving and most grateful; however, despite the fact that you deserve a sentence of death, I do not wish to condemn you; instead, I have decided to give you time for repentance. *Quia nolo mortem peccatoris, sed ut magis convertatur et vivat*,[16] for

[11] Isaiah 9:3.
[12] John 8:10.
[13] John 8:11.
[14] Psalm 22 [23]:4
[15] John 8:11.
[16] A Lenten antiphon drawing on Psalm 93 [94]:19, Ezekiel 33:11 and Mark 2:15-17.

I do not desire the death of sinners nor have I come for that reason, but rather I should like them to reform themselves and to live, for I prefer to be loved than feared, and therefore I say to you: *"Diliges" inquit, non "timeas", quia timere enim servorum est, diligere autem filiorum,*[17] for hereafter may you cast away all fear and begin to serve through love, for I tell you in all certainty that I do not wish to be feared by men as a Master, but rather loved as a Father. So, keep in mind the great benefit you have received, *et amplius noli peccare,*[18] and carry the firm intention in your will never to sin or to offend God again, for you have been in great danger of losing the life of your body and your soul. *Scio tribulationem tuam et inopiam tuam, sed es apud me dives,*[19] for I know your tribulation, and with what pain and suffering you have undergone sin, and how you consider yourself to be poor in merit and devoid thereof, but rest assured that in my presence you are now found to be rich, since you have been worthy of receiving my grace and love. May you know how to keep and preserve it, and do not lose it through your own fault, for if you do so, *erit novissimus error peior priore,*[20] and quite rightly shall you be punished much more severely for your subsequent error than for an earlier one, because it is worse and more blameworthy. Thus, be distrustful of yourself, and take note of the counsel of Solomon, who says: *"Memorare novissima tua, et in aeternum non peccabis",*[21] for, if you are sincerely mindful of your life's end, you shall never have the desire to sin, nor shall you take delight in any aspect of this mortal life if you are mindful of its brevity; you shall exert yourself, rather, with great diligence. *Ante obitum tuum operare iustitiam, quoniam non est apud inferos invenire cibum,*[22] for, if you have not exerted the proper effort here, you shall possess none of it,[23] and for this reason does the devil seek continuous occupation for men, so that they cannot be concerned with providing for the future. *Et tamdiu eos deludat quousque de corpore exeant rei et nudi, et nihil secum praeter peccata portantes.*[24] And thus blinded and deceived to such an extent does he keep them until they leave their bodies in death,

[17] St Thomas Aquinas, *Catena aurea in quatuor evangelia. Expositio in Matthaeum*, Chapter 22, Lesson 4.

[18] John 8:11.

[19] Revelation 2:9.

[20] Matthew 27:64.

[21] Ecclesiasticus [Sirach] 7:40 [36].

[22] Ecclesiasticus [Sirach] 14:17 (Vulgate).

[23] 'It' referring back to God's 'grace and love'.

[24] Jacobus de Voragine, *Legenda aurea*, Chapter II, 'De Sancto Andrea apostolo', ed. Th. Graesse, Leipzig, 1850, p. 16.

and thus blameworthy and laden with sins, and denuded and bare, carrying nothing with them apart from the sad burden of their own sins, does he make them proceed into eternal torment, from which shall be delivered all those who follow and believe in my teaching.'

So the sinner woman, already reformed and fully inflamed, threw herself at the feet of Our Lord, the Son of God, thanking him with unending tears for his immense mercy, and saying: '*Gloria tibi, Domine, qui me vocare dignatus es et cum servis tuis dinumerare*', meaning: 'O Infinite Majesty, glory and praise be given to you, who with such mercy have chosen to call me and draw me towards your love, and to wish that I should be counted and numbered among those who serve you! I, my Lord, offer and give myself entirely to you in the steadfast desire never to offend Your Majesty!'

And the people, much edified by the method Our Lord had adopted in the deliverance of this woman, and praising his infinite wisdom, said: '*Sic suum sermonem temperavit, ut et legi non contradiceret et pietatem non amitteret; et liberata est mulier iubente misericordia*',[25] meaning: 'O how great is the wisdom of this Lord, who has so disposed his words that he has not contradicted the law nor neglected to make use of compassion, whereby the wretched sinner woman has been set free at the command of the King of Mercy. *Exaltabitur autem Dominus solus in die illa*,[26] for on that day was the Lord alone exalted and praised for his merciful works, while the Pharisees were humiliated and put to shame for their cruelty and malevolence, in keeping with what Isaiah had prophesied about them, when he said: '*Oculi sublimis hominis humiliati sunt, et incurvabitur altitudo virorum*',[27] meaning: 'The eyes of those proud men who thought themselves very lofty are humbled, and their haughtiness is brought low.'

---

[25] Bruno da Segni, *Commentaria in Joannem*, Part I, Chapter VII, 23 (PL 165: 515B).
[26] Isaiah 2:11.
[27] *Idem.*

CXXXVIII

OUR MERCIFUL LORD, realising that his mission was coming to an end, and that the term of his life would soon be over, with courageous spirit forced himself to preach, going every day from Bethany to Jerusalem, presenting himself at the temple, and proclaiming his divine teaching to those who wished to hear it. Even so, ill will was already so widespread among the entire people that very few wished to hear him, but rather they fled from any location where His Majesty was, feeling deeply ashamed to have his friendship.

And, therefore, the holy Apostles and all the others who followed him at that time are fittingly exalted and deservingly rewarded, for great love and faith must have kept them steadfast while they saw Our Lord thus persecuted, whose name nobody dared utter in public.

So, therefore, the nearer Our Lord drew to death and the more his persecution mounted, the fuller by far was the love he showed to his disciples and to those in his service, by revealing great secrets to them and encouraging them to question him concerning the doubts they had, so

---

[1] The poor widow episode draws on Mark 12:41-44.

that he might inform them about these at length before his death. And to all in general did he display his very great charity and his unquenchable thirst for the salvation of souls, attracting them by every possible means. So Our Lord could say: '*Popule meus, quid ultra debui facere tibi et non feci?*',[2] meaning: 'O Jewish people whom I have chosen as my own, why have you disowned me in such a way that you do not wish to hear my teaching? Have you not appreciated or acknowledged the singular benefits I have performed? Above every nation have I exalted you, yet you think only of demeaning me; I wish to give my life for you, yet you will not accept my preaching; everything that I had promised to your ancestors, have I fulfilled in deed, yet you have held none of it dear. I wish to show you, therefore, *quia doleo super*,[3] for I grieve deeply at the loss of you, which shall be irreparable.'

So Our Lord, tormented within his soul at the great callousness and ingratitude of the Jews, and realising that they listened to him with such scant devotion, stopped preaching and sat down on a bench that stood in front of the treasury, which was a chest in which people put the coins they offered to the temple. And in that place were high priests and rabbis who guarded that chest, and those who brought large quantities of gold or silver with which to make such an offering and to put in the said chest, they would welcome with great solemnity and reverence, while preaching openly and telling all those who came there that whoever brought a greater quantity to that place achieved far greater merit.

And while Our Lord was watching this, a poor widow came and placed two copper coins in the said chest, which she had earned by the labour of her hands and of which none more remained in her house. Instead, she had decided to go through the day without eating in order to make that offering to Our Lord; yet the priests who were sitting there made no mention of the said woman, but rather scoffed at what she had given.

But Our Merciful Lord, who fully acknowledged the devotion of women, was not prepared to tolerate the fact that the merit of this singular offering should be kept silent. Rather, he wished that by his divine lips it be praised and commended to the glory of women, whose offerings and alms-giving proceed from such fervent love that, however small they may seem in quantity, are very great in the eyes of Our Lord God and highly

---

[2] A line from one of the improperia sung during the Good Friday service.

[3] *Doleo super te...*: this phrase comes from King David's lamentations for his friend Jonathan (2 Samuel 1:17-27) and his son Absalom (2 Samuel 18:33 and 2 Samuel 19:4); it was used as a medieval antiphon and was set to music.

appreciated by him. So, therefore, Our Majesty said [...][4] wishing openly to show the woman's offering to be so outstanding that it surpassed those of the rich people who had given large sums, and addressing his words to the Apostles, he said: '*Vere dico vobis quia vidua haec pauper plus quam omnes misit*',[5] meaning: 'O my disciples, behold how acutely the intellects of these people are blinded by avarice, insofar as they fail to notice the devotion of those who give offerings or to appreciate their goodwill; they simply praise and approve whoever brings a greater sum of money. Truly, I say to you that this poor widow who has just put the two small coins in the treasury has given much more than all the rich people have, for they give from the surplus they have, but she has given everything she had on which to subsist today. Yet the priests scoff at her because she has given so little, but they have fallen into grave error, and of them has David said: "*Qui habitat in caelis irridebit eos*",[6] for my Father, who dwells and abides in Heaven, ridicules them and holds them in abomination, as if cut off from his grace and love.'

Once he had said this, His Majesty departed from there in order to return to Bethany, and the priests remained so incensed that they would have eaten him alive, had that been possible for them. But when he arrived in Bethany, he was welcomed with singular love and devotion by his excellent mother and by the glorious Magdalene, and all rejoiced greatly at his arrival.

And the kindly Martha quickly prepared dinner, as she knew that he had not eaten, for in the city of Jerusalem there was no one who thought about the health of his royal body or about the repose thereof, but rather they—mainly the elders, who abhorred him with an implacable hatred—wished for his death and destruction. And it is said, therefore, of that desolate city: '*Deserta est a sanctis, deserta a sanctitate, a fide et veritate*',[7] for, on account of its great malevolence, was it forsaken by the holy prophets, whom they killed and persecuted, and more recently was it forsaken and abandoned by the Saint of saints, whom with such cruelty they persecuted and cast out and refused to welcome, and it was, of course, forsaken by all sanctity when it forfeited the presence of His Majesty, and henceforth neither faith nor truth were found therein.

[4] A lacuna in the text.
[5] Mark 12:43.
[6] Psalms 2:4.
[7] See John Wycliffe, *Opus evangelicum*, Book III (*De Antichristo*, Book I), Chapter 26.

Part Three: After the Death of Christ

ON HOW THOSE MOST SINGULAR WOMEN, NAMELY, OUR
VIRTUOUS MOTHER EVE AND THE GLORIOUS SAINT ANNE,
CAME TO KISS OUR LORD'S HAND AND HOW, AFTER EVE
HAD SPOKEN FIRST, THEY WERE WELCOMED BY HIM
WITH GREAT LOVE AND GENTLENESS

CXCVII

THOSE HOLY WOMEN rose to their feet with untold fervour, wishing to go to kiss the hand of and pay homage to Our Lord. First came those two matrons of singular regard, namely, our glorious mother Eve and the virtuous Saint Anne, and, after many curtsies, Eve went on the right-hand side as being worthy of every honour on account of her antiquity and of her being the universal mother of all. And with Saint Michael taking her by the arm, as did Saint Gabriel Saint Anne, did they thus come into the presence of Our Lord accompanied by many women.

And our virtuous mother Eve being the first to kneel, she took the sacred hands of Jesus, kissing them with such sweetness that it could not be described in human language. And she began to speak by saying:

'O my Lord and my God, my Creator and my Redeemer, may boundless thanks be given to you, who with such bounty and compassion have repaired my error! I, Lord, caused my husband to sin and to corrupt the whole of human nature, yet you, Lord, have repaired it and saved it, for no other would have sufficed. I was the one to initiate the sin, and I bore the greatest sorrow for that as long as I lived, as you well know, for, when I saw Adam, my husband, made so miserable on account of my fault, I bore a twofold sadness for both of us.

'And when I found myself abhorred by you, Lord, and cast out of that place of repose and put on the earth that you had created for the animals, over and again would I have been rent by excess of sorrow, had it not been for the consolation given on your behalf by this glorious prince, Saint Michael, who never tired of saying to me that Your Highness would be incarnated in a woman, and from her would you take human flesh, subjecting yourself to infinite pain and suffering and to a cruel death, in order to repair my fault. But even though, Lord, I might have heartily rejoiced at my redemption and that of my children, I regretted in the extreme your pain and suffering, since I believed I was the cause of these. And this torment and suffering accompanied my entire life, for I lamented my sin without the slightest pause, performing on its behalf all the penance I could, allowing myself no reprieve, and hoping to satisfy you by all the means according to which I had offended you. For, when I thought of my great pride, whereby desiring to know all things I was persuaded to violate my obedience to you, I humbled my heart through continuous recollection of my disloyalty, insofar as, having received so many and such singular graces from Your Majesty, I could not abide by a single commandment. And this so humbled my soul, that, very often, pierced through with sorrow, I cast myself to the ground, with the intention of sundering it, in order to humble myself before you to the fullest degree. And remembering that sorrowful meal, I never ate fruit or anything which might give delight to my taste: grasses and water alone were my sustenance.

'O Lord, what pain beyond measure was that I felt when that fateful event occurred wherein my first-born son killed his virtuous brother! For a hundred years was I shut away within a cave cut off from the company of Adam and in continuous and sorrowful lament, on account of the offence caused to you rather than the loss of my sons, though I loved them deeply. And from there would I not have emerged throughout my entire life other than at your command. For, when I thought of how much pain that singular lady and daughter of mine, who was destined to be your mother, would feel when she realised and became aware of your pain and suffering, which you would undergo on account of my sin and fault, I felt such compassion for that lady that I thought I would die. So, fully inflamed by love for her, I begged her that, when you had come into this world, she might remember me and my daughters and obtain mercy and forgiveness for us, and that she might agree to be an advocate for women, whom I had cast into such suffering and wretchedness, and for whom she was destined to act as their Restorer, Mother and Mistress. And with her I conversed continually within my soul; I had no other refuge in my suffering than to invoke her aid, and I advised all my sorrowful daughters to have great devotion to and trust in her.'

So Our Lord, seeing that woman whom he had so wondrously formed with his own hands without the medium of man or of woman, but simply from the rib removed from Adam's side, looked upon her with great pleasure, delighting in her virtuous and gracious words; and, taking her by the hands, he drew her very close to him and said to her most lovingly: '*Veni, amica mea, veni et coronaberis*',[1] meaning: 'Come, venerable mother, most beloved by me; come close to me and you shall be crowned as your virtuous repentance deserves, for your sorrows are over. Now begins your happiness and joy, which shall have no end; your sin has now been pardoned and forgiven. Henceforth you shall speak to your daughters, here present, only of delights and pleasures, in the awareness that you are all so beloved and glorified by me. Great has been your sin, and a great redeemer have you deserved by means of your wholesome repentance. And if you have caused great harm to the world by your sin, I have made it all the more beautiful and all the more noble by my suffering and death, and those who are saved after that sin shall have all the more glory on account of the worthiness of my suffering, upon which shall be founded all the endeavours of the elect. And by this example of my death many shall accept martyrdom and shall achieve outstanding levels of glory; not only men, but also women, with immense courage shall dare to lose their lives in order to attain the great honour of martyrdom. And then shall you be most joyful and happy about those singular and virtuous daughters when you learn that they are so loved and cherished by me, on account of their great deeds, inasmuch as they surpass men in the strength of their love.

'And I have given my mother, therefore, as Leader and Lady to these women, in order to protect and defend them from those who seek to speak ill of them. And I wish you to be held in great reverence and devotion by men and women, as the unique mother of all, and for you continually to act on their behalf as intercessor in my presence, and particularly on behalf of women, on whom I shall bestow innumerable graces, out of love

---

[1] Deriving from the Song of Solomon 4:7-8 (Vulgate).

for you, if I learn that they hold you in singular devotion and reverence. For I have instructed those to honour their mother who wish to live long in the love of my grace; and through Solomon have I said: "*Generatio quae matrem suam non benedicit non est lota sordibus*",[2] for children who do not honour their mother cannot be free from great blame. And Solomon himself, inspired by me, fearing that men should be ungrateful to you and should stray from their devotion to you, told them: "*Qui fugit matrem ignominiosus erit et infelix*",[3] in other words, whoever parts from or flees his mother, shall be, among people, filled with great wretchedness and shame. And he explains why, by saying: "*Sapiens mulier aedificat domum suam; os suum aperuit sapientiae, et lex clementiae in lingua eius; panem otiosa non comedit; surrexerunt filii eius et beatissimam praedicaverunt*",[4] meaning that, truly, the wise and sensible woman builds and exalts her household; when she opens her mouth she spills forth wisdom, and the law of clemency is set on the tongue of the virtuous woman, and her prudence does not allow her to eat her bread idle. And the sons of such a mother, being most happy, bless and praise their virtuous mother, wishing to spread throughout the entire world her exceptional reputation. So stand quite assured, therefore, that whoever remembers you, who are universal mother of all, and follows the example of your penitence, shall be generously rewarded by me, while those who speak ill of women shall fall under my wrath, for all of them are capable of understanding that my mother is a woman who has won a great honour for all your daughters, and offers such a strong safeguard to them that nobody can cause affront to them who does not also greatly offend me.'

So, having heard Our Lord and seen his gentleness and compassion, our glorious mother Eve fell down at his feet and kissed them, in her heart more grateful than words could convey for the great mercy and warm welcome she had found in His Majesty.

And the holy angels who were there present, having seen Our Lord speak to that woman, who had been the one to initiate sin, with such familiarity and love, were most delighted at the reconciliation and friendship between them. So, as was their custom—for of them is it said: '*Gaudium est angelis Dei super uno peccatore*',[5] since the angels are singularly joyful at the repentance of a sinner—, they began to say with respect to our glorious

---

[2] An abridgement of Proverbs 30:11-12.

[3] Cf. Proverbs 19:26 (Vulgate).

[4] A conflation of Proverbs 14:1 and Proverbs 31:26-28.

[5] Luke 15:10.

mother Eve, addressing their words to those who lived in the world: *'Honorare illam, peccatores, et impetrabit vobis misericordiam et salutem et pacem'*. And by this they meant: 'O sinners, do not forget this venerable mother of yours, for she meets with such approval from Our Lord and God that by entreaty can she very readily obtain mercy, salvation and peace for you!'

So, once our virtuous mother had risen to her feet, she withdrew a little to make room for the lady who had come with her.

ON HOW THE HOLY AND MOST VIRTUOUS WOMEN, ARRIVING
IN PAIRS, WORSHIPPED AND GLORIFIED OUR LORD, AMONG
WHOM THE COURAGEOUS JUDITH PRAISED AND EXTOLLED
HIS MAJESTY'S GREAT VICTORY

CXCIX

AFTERWARDS THOSE other women came in pairs, with great reverence, in order to worship Our Lord, and each of them individually was warmly welcomed by His Majesty.

And among these others came those two most illustrious ladies who had set his people free, namely, the great and victorious Lady Judith and the most prudent Queen Esther. And, while approaching Our Lord and worshipping His Majesty, Judith, who came first, said: 'O Lord and Eternal King, you are he in virtue of whom I overcame the great tyrant Holofernes, for a woman's strength was not sufficient to deliver your people from such tyranny and oppression. So, therefore, granting the honour of victory to you, I said in my canticle,[1] inviting all the people from the city of Bethulia, delivered by your power alone: "Rejoice, you all, and call upon the name of Our Lord, for he is the breaker of battles and his name is Lord, Our Saviour and Deliverer".'[2]

[1] I.e. The Book of Judith, Chapter 16.
[2] Cf. Judith 16:1-5.

So Our Lord, who was well aware of the virtue of this woman, rejoicing deeply at her arrival and heartily delighted by her virtuous words, said to her: 'O Judith, glory of widows, in the world have you had an eminent reputation on account of your honest and virtuous life, for of you has it been said: "*Non est talis mulier super terram in aspectu, in pulchritudine et in sensu verborum*",[3] in other words, in your time, there did not exist such a woman in the entire world, either in terms of bearing or beauty or wisdom of speech. I now wish you to be praised and extolled much more loftily in my glory, where you shall receive the reward your kindly deeds deserve, for great is the merit owed to those who labour and watch over the public good. So to you, therefore, who risked your life to deliver my people, I desire to be given a power against all demons, so that you may vanquish and overcome them and deliver from their control all those who turn to you in recollection of your strength and victory.'

So the holy angels who were present, seeing the great authority Our Lord had bestowed on this woman, began to sing her praises, using the words: '*Potentia et virtus in brachio tuo, robur et fortitudo in dextera tua*',[4] meaning: 'O glorious woman, great is the power and strength of your arm, and singular force and vigour lie in your right hand.'

So the virtuous woman, finding herself in this manner beloved by Our Lord and extolled by the angels, fell down at the feet of His Majesty, thanking him for his sweetness and compassion in thus having seen fit to reward the services rendered him by his creatures. Once this lady had risen to her feet, then, she kissed Our Lord's hand once more and, having taken leave of His Highness, she withdrew a little in order to make room for the other lady who had come in her company.

[3] Judith 11:19 (Vulgate); 11:21 (RSV-CE).
[4] *Psalterium maius beatae Mariae virginis*, 35; often attributed to St Bonaventure.

ON HOW THE MOST PRUDENT QUEEN ESTHER THANKED
OUR LORD FOR HIS MERCIFUL ADVENT, AND HOW SHE
WAS ROUNDLY PRAISED BY HIM FOR BEING THE
PREFIGURATION OF HIS GLORIOUS MOTHER; AND ON
HOW THE OTHER WOMEN WERE LIKEWISE VERY WARMLY
RECEIVED BY HIS MAJESTY

CC

SO THE HUMBLE and virtuous Queen Esther approached and, worshipping Our Lord's Majesty, she kissed his hands with great sweetness and love, saying to him: 'O infinite clemency, how very welcome you are! How impatiently did all those present await your arrival. I, Lord, when I presented myself to King Ahasuerus, my husband, with the aim of setting free the Jewish people from whom I descended, fainted when I saw the ferocity of his expression; yet now, Lord, seeing the agreeable cast of your genial features, I am filled with inestimable joy, and I thank you for this visitation and for all the other mercies performed for me and for all of human nature.'

So Our Lord, looking at her most lovingly, said to her: 'O Esther, you have been likened to my mother, and therefore it is said of you: "*Erat enim formosa valde, et incredibili pulchritudine, omnium oculis gratiosa et amabilis videbatur*",[1] for you were exceedingly fair, and your beauty was beyond

---

[1] Esther 2:15 (Vulgate).

belief, and therefore you were considered attractive and desirable in the eyes of all your beholders. And thus, if on account of your loveliness and beauty you have been so beloved of and appealing to King Ahasuerus, how much more can you imagine that my most honourable mother is loved and adored by me, of whom I have said through Solomon: "*Tota pulchra es, amica mea, et macula non est in te*",[2] for her beauty is complete and without rival, and in no way can any blemish come near her. She surpasses in excellence any mere creature, and there exists no grace which may be communicated to human nature that has not been given to her in great abundance.

'If King Ahasuerus, by the mercy of his royal nature alone, was unable to allow you, his wife and queen, to come under the universal and common law founded by him, but said to you rather: "*Non enim pro te, sed pro omnibus haec lex constituta est*",[3] meaning that not for you, who were his wife, but for all men was that law constituted and ordained, from which with good reason should you be exempted as his queen greatly beloved by him, how much more have I, who am by nature merciful and almighty, preserved my mother from that common law I founded when angered by Adam's sin, whereby all children descending from him should be conceived in sin, which law was not applicable to my mother. Rather, I tell you, it is a most wretched mind that believes the contrary, and whoever wishes to equate her in any respect to other creatures is coarse of nature, and whoever cannot distinguish between one person and another is more brute animal than human being, for she to whom such rank is communicated as to be my mother should not be equated to others, but instead exalted, praised and extolled above all, for of her is it said: "*Nec primam similem visa est, nec habere sequentem.*"[4]

'So you, Esther, who during your life have rested so firmly upon the virtue of humility, shall be highly exalted by me and honourably crowned in my glory. For stand assured that what is written about me is completely true, namely that: "*Deus superbis resistit, humilibus autem dat gratiam suam*",[5] for God opposes the proud as his enemy, but gives his grace in abundance to those who are merely humble. And I am very sure that you, Queen Esther, have placed your love and trust in me, as is evident from your bouts of anguish and torment during which you turned to me and

[2] Song of Solomon 4:7.
[3] Esther 15:13 (Vulgate); 15:10 (RSV-CE).
[4] A verse from the *Genuit puerpera Regem* antiphon.
[5] James 4:6; 1 Peter 5:5.

said with great confidence: "*Spem in alio nunquam habui praeter in te, Deus Israel.*"[6] And, therefore, from all such torments did I miraculously deliver you, and, now that you are in repose and glory, I wish you to be able to assist all those who turn to you in their tribulation, for those who trust in me with true sincerity not only obtain through entreaty what they ask for themselves but also for anyone else.'

So the angels, hearing Our Lord speak thus with such compassion, and seeing him reveal such love for this woman on account of her humility, which in the eyes of His Majesty is most pleasing, wished to encourage all those alive within the world to follow the example of this holy woman, so they began to sing the following words: '*Beati imitatores humilitatis illius; beati participes caritatis illius; beati perscrutatores virtutum illius; beati conformes benignitatis cordis illius*', with the aim of telling them: 'O how blessed shall be those who imitate the humility of this excellent woman! And truly may those be called blessed who participate in her charity, and greatly may those rejoice who go in search of her virtue. And singularly blessed shall be those who with all their efforts endeavour to conform to the sweetness and kindness of heart which characterise this lady!'

So the glorious Esther, humbling herself before that fount of compassion from which all virtues proceed, after having thrown herself at Our Lord's feet, thanked him as much as she could for his mercy and compassion since he had seen fit to give such a great reward for such meagre efforts.

So, taking leave of Our Lord, Esther, in the company of Judith, went to sit down on the dais with the other ladies.

And afterwards, all the remaining women came to worship His Majesty, Our Lord. Once this worship was over, all of the ladies being most elated at the great welcome and attention His Majesty had shown them, they strove to praise and extol Our Lord and to speak with great delight about the excellent qualities and singular works of His Highness; and so they gazed upon his person in indescribably joyful repose.

---

[6] A Latin ecclesiastical chant dating from at least the tenth century and usually sung on the Feast of Esther.

CCI

SO THE WOMEN—who by nature are more loving than men, since nothing that needed to be remembered for them to satisfy their obligation to love God had been neglected—said among themselves: 'O if only we could see the body of Our Lord, which still hangs on the Cross!' So all of them, anxious to obtain this grace, approached our glorious mother Eve, whom they all revered as their mother, graciously asking her if she would make an entreaty to Our Lord in this respect.

And the glorious Eve, greatly pleased and eager for such a sight, wished to give the honour of such a singular request to her husband, so rising to her feet, she approached Adam, who had taken his seat before everyone else, and said to him: 'Adam, my lord, be so good as to entreat His Majesty, Our Lord, with me, that he might, among the other mercies and graces he has performed for us, allow us to see his holy body before it is taken down from the Cross.'

So Adam, rising very swiftly from his chair, took Eve by the hand in order to go to make the said entreaty, and, having arrived before Our Lord, and knelt down in his presence, Adam said: 'O infinite clemency, to whom all things are possible, may Your Majesty please grant that we and all those here present might be able to see your excellent body, which still hangs on the Cross, so that we might be more ardent and inflamed in our love and reverence for you when we see with our own eyes the suffering and hardship you have undergone for the sake of our redemption!'

And Our Lord, with a very joyous expression, replied by saying: 'Adam, I am very happy to fulfil your request out of indulgence for the two of you and for your daughters, who have been the ones to initiate this request.'

So immediately a path was made from where they stood all the way to Mount Calvary. And without leaving that place, it seemed to them as if they were all gathered around the Cross and could see the body of Our Lord very clearly while worshipping him with profound humility, for his divine nature never left that holy body; rather, it always accompanied his soul and his body, even though these had been separated by death. So, for this reason, that excellent body should be worshipped by latria,[1] and thus was it done by all those glorious saints.

---

[1] From the Greek word λατρεια, meaning 'service, service to God, divine worship'; i.e. the highest form of worship, due to God (i.e. the Holy Trinity) alone, as opposed to 'hyperdulia', which is reserved for the Blessed Virgin, and 'dulia' (Gk. δουλεια, meaning 'veneration'), which is applicable to the saints.

CCV

SO OUR MOTHER Eve turned to face the Mother of God—who still lay there, in a torpor—and threw herself at the latter's feet, kissing them with such love and devotion that it was impossible to gauge, and, drawing herself up, took those glorious hands and kissed them over and again, while beholding Our Lady's inestimable beauty. Yet even though Our Lady lay lifeless, being filled with such pain, Her Royal Highness could not fail to register this outstanding gesture.

Eve then kissed her on the lips with great sweetness, saying: 'O glorious one, my daughter are you by nature, my Mother and Mistress by virtue! What would I or my daughters have done if it were not for the amends you made? What pain and suffering you have undergone, my Lady, in order to repair my error! During the period when I was alive, I dwelt greatly upon your suffering, which had been revealed to me, and I shed so many and such continuous tears over it that all the flesh on my face was burnt by the constant stream of tears. Now, my Lady, I am not in a condition to feel pain or sadness at the divine sight of your son, who has glorified us all; I simply wish to thank and ceaselessly to praise your great sweetness and compassion since you have managed to obtain such glory for us. I have cast my daughters into suffering and wretchedness; you, my Lady, have exalted and dignified them so greatly that as a result of your love alone shall they be esteemed by everyone, for much greater honour shall be paid to them than to men. I entrust them to you, my Lady; take them as your servants, for I am their mother and sincerely love them, and it seems to me that they cannot be placed anywhere as profitably as in your service. And may my daughters who exist—and shall exist—on this earth be certain that in no matter can they oblige me as much as in serving and loving you well. And for those who do so, shall I be the perpetual advocate before God's presence, and to them shall I give my daily blessing while tenderly entrusting them to you once more, and kissing your hands on behalf of each one of them.

Our mother Eve, therefore, turning to face all the daughters who were in her company, instructed them to come and curtsy before and to kiss the hand of their Lady and Leader.

On how the glorious Saint Anne begged her holy
daughter to draw strength from her suffering, and
how the other holy women kissed Our Lady's hands

CCVI

The glorious Saint Anne arrived first, and approached her much beloved daughter, embracing her so tightly that it seemed as if she sought to admit her within her own soul. She then kissed her on the lips, eyes and hands, looking upon her face so lifeless and distraught, and said: 'O dearly beloved daughter of mine, how visibly is the suffering you have undergone displayed upon your face! O daughter and lady of mine, come the day when you shall have left behind the wretchedness of this world and I shall see you reign in Paradise in body and soul, in accordance with what your son has promised, your son who has decided that you should stay on this earth for some time in order to preserve believers in their faith! And, since His Majesty has ordained it, you, my lady and daughter, should patiently bear it, for I have no doubt at all that countless sufferings shall accompany you for the period you remain in this mortal life, as you recall the agonies you have seen your much beloved son undergo, and your regret at the sight of him shall be a ceaseless torment to you.'

So, kissing her over and over again, she said to her: 'O my daughter, rejoice and spend this period of time patiently, since I am certain of the degree to which you are loved by the King of Glory, your son, as well as cherished by every angelic nature and by all your ancestors who are here contemplating your countenance, anxious to see you in glory. So rest assured that we—they and I—shall beseech His Divine Majesty that he might see fit to shorten the duration of your pilgrimage so that you may attain the joy, so fully desired by you, of being inseparably united to the company of your greatly beloved son, and then, my Lady, shall all your suffering be eliminated, in which suffering you have been cloaked and covered for so long now.'

CCXLI

VERY EARLY in the morning on Sunday, the Magdalene left the house to carry out her loving wish to perform some kind of service for the dead body of her Lord and Master, whom she no longer expected to see alive. She was carrying precious ointments in order amply to be able to anoint him and, while handling and touching him, to shed copious tears and to end her sorrowful life alongside him. And the two Marys who were sisters[1] of Our Lady accompanied her, for, just as the three bore a single name, so did they coincide in sorrow and love.

And as they made their way, they came across the places where they had seen Our Lord undergo some kind of torment, and there, as they recalled his suffering, they shed tears of sorrow. And when they passed in front of the Cross where Our Lord had been tortured and died, and the most fervent Magdalene saw it, they all began to weep again while she, with loving fervour, ran to embrace the said Cross. Fit to burst as she stood

---

[1] Mark 16:1 mentions Mary Magdalene, Mary, the mother of James, and Salome; Matthew 27:56 mentions the first two Marys and omits any reference to Salome; John 19:25 mentions the Virgin Mary's sister, 'Mary the wife of Clopas' at the Crucifixion, but at 20.1, the discovery of Jesus' Resurrection, only Mary Magdalene.

there, she lost the power of speech completely, no longer feeling anything but sorrow and torment.

So the other Marys, though they felt great sorrow, had to force and to comfort the Magdalene, fearing that she might die altogether, and they implored her to leave that place in order to continue their journey; and thus with great difficulty they took her away from there.

As they went along, they remembered the huge and heavy stone that they had placed at the mouth of the cave where the tomb lay, so they said to each other: '*Quis revolvet nobis lapidem ab ostio monumenti?*',[2] meaning: 'O how can we not have thought of bringing with us people likely to be able to remove the large stone from the door of the tomb, for a group of frail women will not suffice to apply such a degree of force?'

O the courageous Magdalene, who saw no difficulty in its being carried out, quickened her step believing that she alone would suffice to remove the stone and bring the body out of the tomb, while the other Marys followed her!

And, when they were close to the tomb, they looked and saw that the stone had been moved away from the door and cast on the ground, so with great courage they entered the sepulchre, and there did they see, on the right-hand side, an angel in human form, dressed in white, at the sight of which they were very afraid.

So the angel, observing the distress of the devout women, and wishing to calm them down, with a joyous expression told them: '*Nolite expavescere; Iesum quaeritis Nazarenum, crucifixum: surrexit, non est hic, ecce locus ubi posuerunt eum*',[3] meaning: 'O virtuous ladies, do not be frightened, for I am here to proclaim good news to you and to assure you that Our Lord Jesus of Nazareth, who died on the Cross, and whom you so lovingly seek, has already been resurrected and is not here. Look at the place where they laid him and you shall see that he is not there.'

But such was the sorrow and anguish of the holy women when they did not find the body of Our Lord in the tomb, as they had expected, that they could neither believe nor appreciate the angel's words. Instead, as if beside themselves, they went away, each in her own direction, tearful and sorrowful beyond description, no longer knowing what to do, and losing the hope of finding him, for love is ever fearful of losing what it has, and all the more should it be uncertain of recovering what it has lost. And, therefore, these kindly women had very good reason to grieve.

[2] Mark 16:3.
[3] Mark 16:6.

On how the seraphic Magdalene, remaining at the
tomb in unending tears and sorrow, earned the
right to be comforted by the presence of her
beloved master, who made his first appearance
to her

CCXLII

So the very resilient Magdalene remained steadfast and decided to
die there in the tomb, for it did not seem to her as if anything might rid her
of the pain she was feeling apart from death alone, since she had lost him
who was the life of her soul. She wholly abhorred the life of the body and
wished to expire, thinking that only after she had died would she find what
she had lost whilst alive.

While she thus remained there outside the tomb, she shed unending
tears and tormented herself; so, unable to find any relief from her boundless sorrow, she said: 'O my Lord and my Life, how great was the sadness I
felt at your death! I was still left with some comfort, however, namely that
I could see and handle your dead body. And when I laid you, Lord, in the
tomb, I was fit to burst, yet the hope of being able to anoint you and to
perform some service upon your body helped to relieve my sorrow
somewhat. What shall I do, Lord, now that I lack everything? What
comfort shall I draw, Lord, from such a sorrowful loss?' And thus weeping,
the kindly Magdalene bent down and looked inside the tomb.

But, seeing the place where they had laid the body of her Lord and
Master, and realising that he was not there, a knife of sorrow pierced her

soul once more,[1] and she said with a loud cry: '*Magnus ergo dolor me flere compellit, magna tristitia viscera mea coactat*',[2] meaning: 'Great and boundless sorrow compels me to weep, and a profound and innermost sadness grips and torments my heart.'

So, saying this, she looked again upon that place from which she could not avert her eyes, hoping to see what she could not see; but, tormented by sorrow, once more she began to weep, that sorrow becoming steadily greater as she grew completely dismayed. But Our Lord, who loved her sincerely, sent her two angels in order to console her, angels who spoke to her with very affable expressions, saying: '*Mulier, quid ploras?*',[3] meaning: 'O woman who seems so heartbroken, tell us why you weep to such great excess, in case we can relieve your sorrow, since we have come here for that purpose.'

But the Magdalene, seeing the angels, drew no comfort or relief from her sorrow; instead, as her tears continued, she said: 'Alas, how wretched I am! For I do not seek angels nor do I wish consolation from them; I am searching, rather, for the Lord of Angels, yet him I do not find nor can I see! Who can comfort me after such a loss? Not any created thing, since these instead all cause me distress; my only remedy is to weep and to lament the absence of my Lord, and no other company do I desire, since his, so beloved, have I lost, and here, alone in his tomb, do I seek to end my life.'

The Magdalene, realising that the angels were awaiting her reply, yet wishing them to be gone from there and not to hinder her tears, raised her head slightly and let out a sigh which suggested that her heart would burst, saying: '*Quia tulerunt Dominum meum, et nescio ubi posuerunt eum*',[4] meaning: 'O glorious spirits, if you are angels, as you seem to be, how can you not know the cause of my sorrow? Why do you seek to increase my suffering by asking me to put into words my very grievous loss, for they have taken my Lord away from here and I do not know nor can I tell where they have laid him? Can you bear to hear of greater sorrow? Can any suffering be compared to mine?'

Yet while the Magdalene was saying such things, her beloved Lord was standing behind her, observing with great joy the constancy and fervour of her love, so the angels, seeing Our Lord, prostrated themselves on the ground, worshipping His Majesty.

---

[1] For this same image, see above Chapter XCI.
[2] Bruno da Segni, *Commentaria in Joannem*, Part III, Chapter XX, 52 (PL 165: 593B).
[3] John 20:13.
[4] *Idem.*

So the Magdalene, in awe of the person to whom such singular and profound reverence was being shown, turned around and saw Jesus, her beloved, dressed in disguise, but she did not recognise him; instead, she supposed him to be the gardener. *O Maria, si quaeris Iesum, quare non cognoscis ipsum?* O Mary, where is your good sense? Has your sorrow made you so distraught that you seek Jesus yet, having him before you, you fail to recognise him?

So Our Lord, in order to arouse in her greater desire, delayed revealing his identity to her, and said to her: '*Mulier, quid ploras? Quem quaeris?*',[5] meaning: 'O woman, tell me why you are weeping and what you seek.'

So she, thinking that he who had seemed to her to be the gardener must know where lay the holy body of her Lord that she sought, said to him: '*Domine, si tu sustulisti eum, dicito mihi ubi posuisti eum et ego eum tollam*',[6] meaning: 'O gardener, Sir, why do you ask the reason for my weeping and my seeking? So considerable is it, and so great, that it defies description or being put into words. If you know anything about it, I implore you not to make me suffer; Sir, if you have removed from here that which I seek, I ask you, please, to think fit to tell me, and I shall take it away with me.'

'O Magdalene, what are you saying? Have you forgotten that you are a woman, and very frail by nature? How can you take hold of the dead body, so large and so magnificent, and carry it such a long distance? Are you afraid of nothing? Do you not realise that you are in enemy territory and that you cannot go anywhere without being seen and discovered by the Jews, and that, when they find you with such booty, you shall not escape death? Have you already forgotten the occasion of last Friday, when the great and courageous nobleman so favoured at court, Joseph of Arimathea, did not dare to take down from the Cross this glorious body that you seek without permission from Pilate, yet, even so, the Jews have imprisoned him for having buried it? What do you expect them to do to you if you are accused of having stolen it? O great is your constancy, glorious Magdalene, whereby nothing frightens you! Rightly may it be said of you: "*Quia ferventer amanti nihil videtur difficile*",[7] for he who loves fervently considers no thing difficult in the pursuit of what he desires!

O Magdalene, persevere and do not hesitate, since the Lord for whom you ask is so compassionate that he is never indifferent to anyone who

---

[5] John 20:15.
[6] *Idem.*
[7] Found in Cicero, *Orator* 10.33, *amanti nihil difficile* is a common Latin maxim.

loves him, nor does he withdraw from anyone who fondly seeks him. Do you know what His Majesty is very often in the habit of doing? *Occultat se ut ardentius requiratur, et requisitus cum gaudio inveniatur, et inventus cum sollicitudine teneatur, et tentus non dimittatur,*[8] for he conceals himself so that he be ardently sought and, once sought, that he be joyfully found, and once found, that he be retained and preserved with great solicitude, and once retained, that he be preserved with singular care and on no account forsaken.'

So Our Lord, observing the Magdalene, and seeing that her sorrow was so great that if he did not help her without delay she would lose her life completely, decided to reveal his identity to his beloved, so he said to her with his customary gentleness of speech: 'Mary'.

And she, hearing herself named by the one she loved so much, let out a great cry of extreme joy, and said: 'O my Lord and Master, you are the one I seek! I have found you, my Life!' And she fell at His Majesty's feet so as to kiss them.

But he said to her: '*Noli me tangere, nondum enim ascendi ad Patrem meum*',[9] 'Magdalene, I do not wish you to touch me bodily until you sincerely believe me to be equal to my Father. *Potius volo ut tangas me tactu mentis, credens me Patri aequalem, quam tactu corporis, me credens hominem purum et Patre minorem*',[10] by which Our Lord meant: 'Magdalene, I prefer that you touch me first of all via the contact of your mind, believing me to be equal to my Father, rather than by means of that of your body, believing me to be a mere man and to be less than my Father.'

So the Magdalene, who wished her beloved Lord to be admitted into her soul, felt infinite pain at the fact that she was not allowed to touch him, and in floods of tears said: '*Credo, Domine, adiuva incredulitatem meam*',[11] meaning: 'I, Lord, firmly believe that you are God eternal, and equal to your Father. Help me, merciful Lord, and forgive my unbelief, for extreme love, Lord, has made me doubt, for so much did I desire your Resurrection that it seemed to me that I was bound never to see it, and I considered myself content with simply being in possession of and holding your dead body! Let me touch it now, Lord, since you have shown it to me both living and immortal!'

---

[8] Auctor incertus (Ps.-Bernardus Claraevallensis; attributed to Drogo, possibly the abbot of St John, Laon, †1137), *Meditatio in passionem et resurrectionem Domini*, XV, 38 (PL 184: 766B).

[9] John 20:17.

[10] Ludolph of Saxony, *Vita Jesu Christi*, Part 2, Chapter 72, §7.

[11] Mark 9:23 (Vulgate); 9:24 (RSV-CE).

O amor fortis et impatiens! Non enim sufficiebat ei videre Iesum et cum Iesu loqui, nisi etiam tangeret Iesum,[12] for the Magdalene's most fervent love could not patiently accept that she should have to content herself simply with seeing and speaking to Jesus, but rather wished to touch Jesus, her beloved.

Our Merciful Lord, being aware of the Magdalene's great longing, wished to make her entirely happy, however, so His Majesty allowed her to kiss his feet and hands, as she had been hoping, and he embraced her with the greatest love, saying to her: '*O Maria! Magna est constantia tua, magna est fides tua; ideo meruisti quem mortuum quaerebas vivum videre et audire*',[13] meaning 'O Mary, my disciple and my beloved, great and singular is your constancy, and great and perfect is your faith! So, therefore, you have fittingly deserved that he whom you sought when he was dead, have you seen and heard alive.'

And the seraphic Magdalene, remaining at the holy feet of Jesus, felt an indescribable sweetness, and said: '*Te cupio, diligo et adoro, cum quo manebo, regnabo et beata ero*',[14] meaning: 'O Lord, you are the one I love and cherish! I adore you, Lord, with all the depths of my soul! I am with you, o infinite clemency, and, for me, being in the company of Your Majesty is to reign; and more blessed do I count myself, having attained so much mercy and grace from you!'

So Our Lord lingered there for a while in order to comfort the Magdalene. *Stant ergo dilecti cum iocunditate et gaudio magno loquentes ad invicem sicut amicus cum amico*.[15] And the two of them, Jesus and the Magdalene, who loved each other sincerely, experienced great happiness and joy beyond description, talking just like one friend to another.

But Our Lord, having comforted and cheered the Magdalene by his presence, wished to bid her farewell, so he embraced her once more while giving her his blessing at length; and she, with profound humility, worshipped His Majesty by kissing his feet.

And, once Our Lord had departed, the Magdalene was left with a very great sense of loss.

[12] Ludolph of Saxony, *loc. cit.*
[13] *Ibid.*, §5.
[14] St Anselm of Canterbury, *Liber meditationum et orationum*, XIV, 3 (PL 158: 781D).
[15] Ludolph of Saxony, *Vita Jesu Christi*, Part 2, Chapter 72, §8.

ON HOW OUR LORD APPEARED A SECOND TIME TO THE
HOLY WOMEN WHO WERE RETURNING FROM THE TOMB,
WHICH WOMEN, BY SINGULAR PRIVILEGE, HE INSTRUCTED
TO PROCLAIM HIS RESURRECTION TO THE APOSTLES

CCXLIII

So, FINDING herself alone, the glorious Magdalene remembered the virtuous Marys who had come with her and of whom, amid her great anguish and unease, she had never been conscious or known the whereabouts.

Thus, emerging from that cave which lay in front of the tomb, she searched for them throughout the orchard. Failing to locate them, however, she went outside and, looking around, saw them close to the hedges surrounding the said orchard, each at a distance from the other, and intensely distraught, so she said to them: 'O ladies, rejoice and feel infinite delight, *quia vidi Dominum*,[1] for you may be sure that I have seen the Lord resurrected from death into life.'

And, though greatly delighted by what they had heard, they were extremely upset by the fact that they had not heard it themselves, so all

[1] John 20:18.

three of them decided to return to the Cenacle.² So, along the way, the two Marys first of all questioned the Magdalene as to the circumstances in which she had seen Our Lord and to what he had said to her. While she was recounting it all in detail, however, Our Lord himself came to meet them, and said to them with a very joyous expression: '*Avete.*'³

The holy women, therefore, recognising His Majesty, prostrated themselves on the ground and worshipped him. And they took hold of his feet and hands, and with infinite joy they kissed them over and again, being completely convinced of his Resurrection. '*Primo mulieres merentur audire "avete", ut maledictum Evae mulieris in mulieribus solveretur.*'⁴ And not without great mystery have women deserved first of all to hear such a greeting, namely, '*avete*', Our Lord plainly showing thereby that the curse laid upon the first woman, who was Eve, had now been completely lifted from womankind.

And the said women stayed there a short while, conversing with the Lord with untold delight, marvelling at his glorious presence.

But His Majesty, wishing to leave them, said: '*Ite et annuntiate fratribus meis*',⁵ meaning: 'Go, my beloveds, for more than anything else, I wish you, as women, to be those who proclaim my Resurrection, and that my brethren, namely, the Apostles, hear it from you, so that all the world should know that whoever is more ardent in love deserves to be first in happiness, comfort and favour, as they shall see from experience in you.'

The holy women, realising that Our Lord was instructing them to depart from his presence, were distraught at having to leave such company, so throwing themselves at His Majesty's feet, they said: '*O dulcissime, benignissime, amantissime, carissime Domine, quis nos separabit a te?*',⁶ meaning: 'O sweet, gracious, kindly and dear Lord, who shall separate us from you? For, although it is very gratifying for us to bear such excellent news to your Apostles and servants, having to part from you brings us great sorrow.'

So Our Lord replied to them most lovingly, saying: 'O Magdalene, and you, my aunts, do not think that I am destined to be with you on earth

² The upper room where the Last Supper took place.
³ Meaning, 'Hail!'.
⁴ St Thomas Aquinas, *Catena aurea in quatuor evangelia. Expositio in Matthaeum*, Chapter 28, Lesson 2.
⁵ Matthew 28:10.
⁶ A conflation of St Augustine (incertus), *Meditationum*, XXXVII (PL 40: 933), and Romans 8:35.

now for as long a time as I was accustomed to being, for you shall receive from me only a few brief appearances designed to elevate your minds towards the thought that it is in heaven that you shall possess me rather than on earth.'

Having said this, Our Lord disappeared, and the women were left alone not without a huge sense of loss, so with great haste they returned to the Cenacle, where Our Excellent Lady was along with all the Apostles.

So, as they were entering through the door, they proclaimed to the said Apostles, who were at the threshold, how they had unmistakably seen the resurrected Lord, and the Apostles, rejoicing with infinite delight at such a singular piece of news, said: '*Mulier, quae fuerat ianua mortis, prima praedicat resurrectionem et ostendit ianuam vitae*',[7] meaning: 'O Lord, how gracious it is that woman, who at the beginning of the world was the entrance and doorway for death, has now, on account of her great rank, been made by you the new preacher of your wondrous Resurrection!'

And with infinite delight the glorious women entered the room of Our Lady and, having thrown themselves to the ground, they repeatedly kissed her feet and hands, being unable to say anything about what they had seen, because of their extreme joy.

And the loving Magdalene, who bore the greater part of their delight, drew strength, since she wished to communicate her joy to Our Lady. She could nevertheless tell from Our Lady's expression that the latter knew all about it and that she had been the first to receive a visitation from Our Lord, her son, as reason demanded. She said to Her Excellency: '*O Domina, cesset igitur omnis amaritudo, quia hodie surrexit Dominus; fugiat mors, quia hodie nobis vita data est*', meaning: 'O merciful Lady, you and we together must refrain from all grief and sorrow, for we are wholly convinced that today Our Lord has been resurrected! My Lady, let death take flight, for today has life been restored to us!'

And her elder sister said to Our Lady: '*O felix femina quae talem et tantum filium habere meruisti*', meaning: 'O blessed woman and Mistress of all women, who has been worthy of having such a son and such a great son! Today you see him glorious and resurrected!'

And the younger sister replied to confirm what the elder one had said, by saying to Our Lady: '*O quantum gloriari potuit cum se tantum ornatam cognoverit*', meaning: 'O, my Lady, what glory and joy can be felt by the per-

---

[7] Bruno da Segni, *Commentaria in Matthaeum*, Part IV, Chapter XXVIII, 105 (PL 165: 311B).

son who is—and is aware of being—adorned with such rank as you possess today! So, Your Highness may be sure that *nulla post illam potest esse illustrior corona quam concipere Deum,* for no other such crown can be found as illustrious as the one you wear on account of your having conceived and given birth to God made man. And by reason of this crown, my Lady, do you deserve all the excellent things that henceforth shall follow, for your principal sorrows, my Lady, have ended, since Our Lord, your son, has been resurrected and human nature redeemed, just as you so dearly wished. *Triumpha igitur, felix, quia ex lacte tuae virginitatis effectus est sanguis nostrae redemptionis.* O Blessed and Excellent Lady, what good reason you have to rejoice and celebrate, for from your virginal milk has undoubtedly been fashioned the blood of our redemption!'

So, delighted at the arrival of the Magdalene and of her sisters and at what they had said about the Resurrection of Our Lord, her son, Our Lady told them with great familiarity about what she had seen, and the inestimable comfort she had received from Our Lord, her son, in compensation for the extreme suffering she had undergone as a result of his death.

So they spent the entire day in these pleasant conversations, and celebrated Holy Easter.

ON HOW OUR LORD CROWNED HIS MOST HOLY MOTHER
WITH THREE MOST EXCELLENT CROWNS GIVEN TO HER AS A
WORTHY EMPRESS BY THE MOST HOLY TRINITY, AND HOW,
WITH INESTIMABLE JOY, ALL ANGELS AND MEN GAVE
PRAISE, HONOUR AND GLORY TO HER

CCLXXXIX

BEFORE OUR LORD and his beloved mother were seated in those stately chairs, His Majesty said to his excellent mother: '*Veni, coronaberis*',[1] meaning: 'Come, my dearest mother, and you shall be crowned by my hand before your departure, with three crowns sent by the entire Holy Trinity, so that my disciples, who are here in their mortal bodies and must remain on earth, may see some part of the glory and excellence that soon you are to possess as a most worthy empress and universal Mistress of all.'

So as the most humble Virgin knelt down before her son and eternal God, there appeared three angels who were among the greatest Princes of Paradise, each of whom was bearing one of the said crowns in a beautiful and highly wrought golden bowl, and kneeling with great reverence before Our Lord's Majesty and that of his holy mother, they offered them to him.

[1] Song of Solomon 4:8.

So, taking the first and most excellent crown, Our Lord placed it on the head of Our Lady, his mother, saying: '*Accipe coronam quam tibi Pater meus praeparavit in aeternum*',[2] meaning: 'My dearest mother, take this crown which His Majesty, my Father, sends to you, who had it fashioned and prepared for you by virtue of his great power before the world was created, so that it be worn by you for the first time today. In this worthy crown are set twelve carbuncles more resplendent than the sun, revealing how with twelve degrees of singular purity you gleam and sparkle above every creature. Upon this crown are strewn an innumerable multitude of pearls of most unusual beauty and size, showing your virtues and excellences to be so many that they cannot be counted or comprehended by anyone but him who has chosen to create you in this way by revealing in you the great magnitude of his divine power. And around this crown are inscribed letters in very costly enamel, disclosing your rank to observers, which letters read:

> *Sol es, virgo, eclipsim nesciens,*
> *Sol in caelis de terra oriens,*
> *Sol de caelis terram prospiciens,*
> *Sol peccati nubes demoliens,*[3]

meaning: so that all who behold and contemplate may know and acknowledge your glory and excellence, whereby you, O Virgin most pure, are the brilliant sun that has never been darkened by the great eclipse of Original Sin, but rather have you always shone absolutely free of all blame. You are the sun which, having emerged from the earth, has shone brightly in the sky.[4] And now shall you rise into the sky and cast the rays of your luminosity upon the earth like a most glorious sun which illuminates the inhabitants thereof, and by the intense heat of this sun shall be destroyed and obliterated the clouds representing the sins of those who shall invoke and call upon you, o bright sun. And therefore my Father wishes you to bear this title upon your excellent crown.'

---

[2] Text from a Gregorian chant: Common of several Virgins, Matins, Nocturn 1, Responsory 1.

[3] Part of a prayer to the Virgin Mary attributed to Petrus Netere of Strasbourg. See C. Blume and G. M. Dreves, *Analecta Hymnica Medii Aevi*, Leipzig, O. R. Reisland, 1899, pp. 188-90.

[4] In Latin, as in Catalan (and other Romance vernaculars), the word *caelus* (Cat. *cel*) signifies 'sky', 'heaven' and 'the heavens'.

So Our Lord and Redeemer, having placed the first crown on the head of his Most Serene Mother, then took the second crown, and placing it on top of the other in order to render it even more beautiful, said to the Virgin most pure: 'Most Holy Mother of mine, out of love for me shall you wear this crown in which are set thirty-three diamonds of most unusual beauty and size, representing the thirty-three years I have remained in the world and during which you have served and accompanied me with such love that it is now fitting that upon your crown should shine forth the infinite merits you deserve for your most virtuous efforts.

'O my Most Excellent Mother, the workmanship on this crown, which I took pleasure in painting and beautifying, is a mirror of my wisdom, and upon it there are twelve thousand and fifty-three[5] enamels of various colours, representing the number of days which passed between the day when I took human flesh from you until the day my life ended. And for the great sorrows you underwent on my account on each of those days, shall you now have infinite joys without end. This crown is made and woven from myrtle leaves, wrought from a most singular gold, which renders your crown more beautiful. And the said leaves number one hundred and forty-four thousand seven hundred and thirty-three[6] for precisely this number of hours passed between the moment when you, o mother of mine, conceived me until that point when, in your presence, I expired on the Cross. And because during each of these hours and the moments thereof your charity has been so ardent and inflamed in serving and loving me that you never ceased to perform services and deeds upon my body, services so lofty and so agreeable to me that they could not be rewarded on earth, now, on this day shall you receive the glory and exaltation that you deserve for such continuous, repeated and ardent works. And with supreme delight shall you be praised and extolled eternally and endlessly by every angelic and human nature. And, therefore, inscribed around this crown, in very bright letters of singular workmanship, are the words: "*Te beatam laudare cupiunt omnes sancti, sed non sufficiunt, nam tot laudes tibi conveniunt, o Maria*",[7] meaning that all the saints, with singular fervour, wish to praise and extol you, o blessed mother of mine, yet they do not succeed in properly explaining your glory and excellence, for to you belongs

---

[5] $365 \times 33 = 12,045 + 8$ (leap years) $= 12,053$ days.

[6] The correct number of hours is (approximately) 295,842 (including leap years and the nine months of Mary's pregnancy).

[7] See Blume and Dreves, *op. cit.*, p. 72.

all the praise that can be uttered, o glorious Mary! For this gracious name of yours, o mother of mine, constitutes the delight and joy of angels and men, and invites them into your service and praise.'

After the Most Humble Virgin had been crowned with two such lofty crowns, Our Lord then took the third crown, which was of singular resplendence and beauty, and said to his excellent mother: 'Most Ardent Mother of mine, the Holy Spirit sends you this crown, as his most worthy bride, so that you appear wearing three crowns in the presence of all your servants who shall be in attendance at this ceremony for you, so that they may know that you are the Great and Most Excellent Empress of Heaven and Earth. On this crown are set fifty very fine blazing rubies in order to represent the fifty days which passed between the time I was resurrected and when I sent the Holy Spirit upon your College, of which you had been Doctor and Rectress, and also because during that period your charity was so exercised in continual prayer requesting and asking for the said advent[8] in order to comfort and strengthen my disciples. So, on account of this, that most ardent charity shall now shine forth from your excellent crown.

'And, in order further to beautify that crown, one hundred and twenty pearls of most unusual beauty and whiteness are placed in singular order, to mark the number of tongues of fire which appeared at the said advent of the Holy Spirit and which separately positioned themselves above the heads of each of those who were in your company, so that it should be perfectly clear to all that the graces and gifts that the Holy Spirit distributes among all those he has chosen and loves, are, in you, o mother of mine, united in very great excellence and singularity. For your soul is disposed and prepared so as to receive the graces and gifts of the Holy Spirit that he heaps and lavishes here below and by which he bestows his riches and magnificence without restraint. For you, o mother of mine, are the chest for his treasure and the very dear home of his repose and joy. And, therefore, around this crown is it written in very finely formed gilt lettering: 'Haec est domus fidelis, hoc immortale templum, in quo Spiritus Sanctus requiescit',[9] with the aim of informing all those who behold or contemplate your most excellent crown that you are the most faithful house and temple of immortal memory in which the Holy Spirit rests and abides with singular pleasure.'

[8] See below.
[9] An adaptation of Lactantius, *Divinae institutiones*, 4:14.

And when the Most Serene Virgin had been thus loftily crowned, Our Lord sat down in the chair which had been prepared for him, instructing Our Lady to sit at his right hand, very close to him, as his singularly beloved mother.

So all the angels and men there present, having been astonished at the level of glory and magnificence they had observed in the Most Excellent Mother of God prior to her departure, and having been convinced that she would not possess a great deal more when she was installed in her kingdom, with supreme joy began to sing before Our Lady the words: '*Laetare, Maria virgo, laetitia inenarrabili in anima et corpore in proprio filio, cum proprio filio, per proprium filium*',[10] meaning: 'Most merciful Mary and purest Virgin, rejoice with untold delight in your soul and your body at your own son, who has prepared such glory for you, and take pleasure, O Lady, in him, whose company you are never in danger of losing! O how great is the glory and happiness that comes to you, O excellent Lady, through Our Lord, your own son! *Quia haec est omnium laetantium pulchrum carmen, omnium regnantium sceptrum rectum, omnium peregrinantium panis vitae, et omnium expectantium merces summa*, for he is the fair and charming song, the true delight, of all who rejoice! His Royal Majesty is the straight, sure and most steady sceptre of all who rule; just as he is the softest bread which imparts life and salvation to the pilgrims of this mortal life; and the supreme payment and most certain reward for all who have trust in his mercy. O my Lady, the joy that you feel at being mother of this most excellent son surpasses all knowledge, angelic or human. And, therefore, my Lady, you alone sense and savour this sovereign delight, while we all rejoice at what we are capable of knowing, and your joy, Most Serene Lady, shall we celebrate eternally in the glory of Paradise, where you shall very soon be installed.

So, having finished their singing, they all came one by one to kiss the hand of the Most Holy Mother of God, who showed to each one an immense amount of love, and took great delight in them.

[10] Jacobus de Voragine, *Legenda aurea*, Chapter CXIX, 'De assumptione beatae Mariae virginis', § 1, ed. cit., p. 511; cf. St Augustine (incertus), *De assumptione beatae Mariae virginis*, VIII (PL 40: 1148).

CCXCI

WITH THE HOUR of dawn approaching, the great prince Saint Michael, being an outstanding Chamberlain, came to kneel down before Our Lord, saying to His Majesty: 'It behoves you, O excellent Lord, to hasten Our Lady's departure, for the entire Kingdom of Paradise is ready to welcome your mother, the Lady Empress, in this new admittance and singular celebration surrounding Her Majesty's royal coronation.'

So, with a very affable expression, Our Lord turned to his Most Holy Mother, and said to her: '*Veni de Libano*',[1] meaning: 'Come, o mother of mine; come away from this great mountain of Lebanon, which is the present world where you have come to seek the grace and original justice that your father Adam had lost! And you found it in all its fullness, as Gabriel told you when he proclaimed my conception to you. For you, dearest mother, are the Great and Most Excellent Cedar planted among the thorns of this mountain, so upright and firm that never has the wind or storm of original, venial or mortal sin been able to separate you for a single moment from the divine grace and love found by you; but rather, since your roots go very deep, on account of your most profound and perfect humility have you risen so high that, the uppermost branches of your charity stretching as far as the heights of Heaven, you have induced me to descend therefrom in order to reaffirm in Adam and in his children the grace found by you.'

[1] Song of Solomon 4:8.

The Reason for the Conclusion and
End of the Present Book

IN KEEPING WITH the elegant style of her royal nature and upbringing,
this illustrious and Reverend Abbess, Mother and Lady,[1] had so very
devoutly and truthfully written the sacred life and death of Jesus, Our
Redeemer and God, and of his Most Honourable Mother. And she had
begun to write, according to her lofty understanding, about the latter's
glorious Assumption, when, during those countless deaths of the year
1490,[2] on Friday 2nd of July, on the Feast of the Visitation of Our Lady, in
the sixtieth year of her virtuous age, her mortal life came to an end, in
order that, by passing into immortal life, she might feel the true experience of the excellence and celebration she had chosen to discuss, and
might receive in Heaven eternal her full reward for the forty-five years so
profitably spent in the present monastery, for twenty-seven of which she
had deservedly been prioress and abbess.

On account of the death and the absence of their abbess, her daughters, maids and subjects remained so filled with irremediable sorrow and
sadness at the extent of the exemplary virtue, religious zeal, wholesome
teaching and famous reputation they had enjoyed by virtue of her much-
loved presence.

---

[1] 'Mother', i.e. the respectful title given to a superior in an order of nuns; 'Lady' on
account of her noble lineage.
[2] Probably referring to the number of fatalities attributable to the plague of that
year, from which Isabel herself died.

However, not only were these women troubled and afflicted by such a loss, but without doubt so was the whole of Spain deprived of a universal and devout mother. And so that it be clear to readers that there exists no other woman who might have the capacity or ability to finish these writings and works begun by a such a great lady, the present book shall close with this conclusion.

May the utility and devotion derived by those who read or recount this book serve to increase the accidental glory of that singular woman who has lent order to it. And to His lofty Divine Majesty, from whom proceed all gifts and graces, may praise, honour, glory and blessing be given by all *in saecula saeculorum. Amen.*

IN PRAISE, HONOUR AND GLORY OF THE MOST HOLY TRINITY WAS
THE PRESENT VITA CHRISTI PRINTED, AT THE BEHEST OF THE
REVEREND SISTER ALDONÇA DE MONTSORIU, ABBESS OF THE MONASTERY
OF THE SISTERS OF THE TRINITY IN THE DISTINGUISHED CITY OF VALENCIA,
AND BROUGHT TO PRESS BY LOPE DE LA ROCA, A GERMAN, AND FINISHED IN THE
SAID CITY, ON THE 22ND OF AUGUST IN THE YEAR OF THE NATIVITY OF OUR LORD

1497

Select Bibliography

ABBREVIATIONS

PL   Jean-Paul Migne, *Patrologiae Latinae Cursus Completus*, 217 vols., 1844-1855

RSV-CE *The Holy Bible*, Revised Standard Version. Catholic Edition, 1965-1966

EDITIONS

Vita Christi de la Reverent Abadessa de la Trinitat, Aldonça de Montsoriu (ed.), Valencia, Lope de la Roca, 1497. Reprint: facsimile edition, 1980; facsimile edition, with an introduction by Albert-Guillem Hauf i Valls, 2006.

Vita Christi de la Reverent Abbadessa de la Trinitat: novament historiat: corregit y smenat per un mestre en sacra theologia, Valencia, Jorge Costilla, 1513.

Vita Christi d[e] la Reverent Abbadessa dela Trinitat corregit ab les cotacions novame[n]t tretes en los marges, Barcelona, Carles Amorós, 1527.

Vita Christi compost per Sor Isabel de Villena, abadessa de la Trinitat de Valencia, ara novament publicat segons l'edició de l'any 1497, 3 vols., Ramon Miquel i Planas (ed.), Barcelona, Biblioteca Catalana, 1916.

Vita Christi, 2 vols., Josep Almiñana i Vallés (ed.), Valencia, Ajuntament de València, 1992.

Partial editions and translations

Parra, Lluïsa (ed.), Isabel de Villena, *Vita Christi*, Biblioteca d'Autors Valencians 12, Valencia, Institució Alfons el Magnànim / Institució Valenciana d'Estudis i Investigació, 1986.

Cantavella, Rosanna & Lluïsa Parra (eds.), Isabel de Villena, *Protagonistes femenines a la* Vita Christi, Barcelona, LaSal (Clàssiques Catalanes, 15), 1987.

Hauf i Valls, Albert-Guillem (ed.), Isabel de Villena, *Vita Christi*, Barcelona, Edicions 62 i La Caixa (Les Millors Obres de la Literatura Catalana, 115), 1995.

Gifreu, Patrick (tr.), Isabel de Villena, *Femmes dans la vie du Christ*, Perpignan, Éditions de la Merci, 2008.

Secondary sources

Alemany Ferrer, Rafael, 'Dels límits del feminisme de la "Vita Christi" de sor Isabel de Villena', in Rafael Alemany, Antoni Ferrando and Lluís B. Meseguer (eds.), *Actes del Novè Col·loqui Internacional de Llengua i Literatura Catalanes*, Barcelona, Publicacions de l'Abadia de Montserrat / Universitat d'Alacant / Universitat de València / Universitat Jaume I, 1993, Vol. 1, pp. 301-313.

Badia i Margarit, A. M., *Les* Regles d'esquivar vocables *i* 'La questió de la llengua', Barcelona, Institut d'Estudis Catalans (Biblioteca Filològica, 38), 1999.

Cantavella, Rosanna, 'Isabel de Villena, la nostra Christine de Pizan', *Encontre* 2 (Winter-Spring 1986), pp. 79-86.

—, 'El feminisme', in *Protagonistes femenines a la* Vita Christi, Barcelona, LaSal (Clàssiques Catalanes, 15), 1987, pp. XIX-XXVII.

Ennen, Edith, *The Medieval Woman*, translated by E. Jephcott, Oxford, Basil Blackwell, 1989.

Ferrante, Joan, *To the Glory of Her Sex: Women's Roles in the Composition of Medieval Texts*, Bloomington, Indiana University Press, 1997.

Fuster, Joan, 'Jaume Roig i Sor Isabel de Villena', in *Obres completes*, Barcelona, Edicions 62, 1968, Vol. 1, pp. 175-210.

Hauf i Valls, Albert-Guillem, 'La *Vita Christi* de Sor Isabel de Villena y la tradición de las *Vitae Christi* medievales', in *Studia in honorem Prof. M. De Riquer*, Barcelona, Quaderns Crema, 1987, Vol. 2, pp. 105-164.

—, *D'Eiximenis a Sor Isabel de Villena: aportació a l'estudi de la nostra cultura medieval*, Valencia, Publicacions de l'Abadia de Montserrat / Institut de Filologia Valenciana (Biblioteca Manuel Sanchis Guarner, 19), 1990.

—, 'Text i context de l'obra de Sor Isabel de Villena', in *Literatura valenciana del segle XV: Joanot Martorell i Sor Isabel de Villena*, Valencia, Generalitat Valenciana / Consell Valencià de Cultura, 1991, pp. 91-124.

—, *La* Vita Christi *de sor Isabel de Villena (s. XV) como arte de meditar: Introducción a una lectura contextualizada*, Valencia, Biblioteca Valenciana / Generalitat Valenciana / Monasterio de San Miguel de los Reyes, 2006.

LABARGE, Margaret Wade, *Women in Medieval Life: A Small Sound of the Trumpet*, London, Hamish Hamilton, 1986.

ORTS MOLINES, J. L., 'A propòsit de "l'estil femení" en Sor Isabel de Villena', in Rafael Alemany, Antoni Ferrando and Lluís B. Meseguer (eds.), *Actes del Novè Col·loqui Internacional de Llengua i Literatura Catalanes*, Barcelona, Publicacions de l'Abadia de Montserrat / Universitat d'Alacant / Universitat de València / Universitat Jaume I, 1993, Vol. 1, pp. 315-325.

MITCHELL, Linda E. (ed.), *Women in Medieval Western European Culture*, New York, Garland, 1999.

PEARSON, Roland, 'Reading Medieval Women: A Case for Translating Isabel de Villena's *Vita Christi*', in Francisco Fernández (ed.), *Los estudios ingleses en el umbral del tercer milenio*, Valencia, Universitat de València (Studies in English Language and Literature. Miscellaneous, 3), 2001, pp. 249-259.

PERNOUD, Régine, *Women in the Days of the Cathedrals*, translated and adapted by A. Côté-Harriss, San Francisco, Ignatius Press, 1998.

PIERA, Montserrat, 'Writing, *Auctoritas* and Canon Formation in Sor Isabel de Villena's *Vita Christi*', *La Corónica* 32, no. 1 (2003), pp. 105-118.

RIQUER, Martí de, *Història de la literatura catalana*, 4 vols., Esplugues de Llobregat, Editorial Ariel, 1964, Vol. 3, pp. 453-484 (reprinted 1980).

ROSENTHAL, Joel T. (ed.), *Medieval Women and the Sources of Medieval History*, Athens, University of Georgia Press, 1990.

ROTELLE, John E. (ed.) & Edmund HILL (tr.), *The Works of St. Augustine: A Translation for the 21st Century*, 20 vols., New York, New City Press, 1991-.

SHAHAR, Shulamith, *The Fourth Estate: A History of Women in the Middle Ages*, London, Methuen, 1983.

SMITH, Lesley & Jane H. M. TAYLOR (eds.), *Women, the Book, and the Godly: Selected Proceedings of the St Hilda's Conference, 1993*, Woodbridge, D. S. Brewer, 1995.

TWOMEY, Lesley K., 'Sor Isabel de Villena: A Gendered Perspective on the Immaculate Conception', *Journal of Catalan Studies* 6 (2003).

—, 'Sor Isabel de Villena: Her *Vita Christi* and an Example of Gendered Immaculist Writing in the Fifteenth Century', *La Corónica* 32, no. 1 (2003), pp. 89-103.

—, 'Poverty and Richly Decorated Garments: A Re-evaluation of Their Significance in the *Vita Christi* of Isabel de Villena', in Robin Netherton and Gale R. Owen-Crocker (eds.), *Medieval Clothing and Textiles*, Woodbridge, The Boydell Press, 2007, Vol. 3, pp. 119-134.

DATE DUE
